MW00973603

The Odyssey

Of

Survival

The Odyssey

Of

Survival

The Odyssey

Of

Survival

Marcia E. Fisher

Barefoot Book Publishers
Ocala, FL
2011

Copyright 2011

TXu001281742/2006-01-18

"The Odyssey Of Survival"

Published by:

Barefoot Book Publishers, Inc.
Email: barefootbookpublishers@yahoo.com
239-249-0108 (USA)
905-428-6746 (Canada)

Cover Photo: Marcia O'Connor-Fisher

ISBN - 978-0-983-6161-0-8

Revamp My Life Ministries, Inc.
Email: info.revampmylife@gmail.com
Website: Revampmylifeministeries.com

"Fear not, for I am with you; be not dismayed,
for I am your God. I will strengthen you, yes,
I will help you, yes, I will uphold you with the
right hand of my righteousness."

Isaiah 41: 10 (KJV)

Memory

I will never forget my beloved Daddy.
The hole in my heart for you is deeper
than the one in which your soft brown eyes
and lips that were always
ready with a smile, lay frozen.
I wish I could see you one more time.
I love you.

Preface

Ilive pretending to be the product of a normal family. I have
formed a web, creating a world of my own, in which I have
severed, or in many instances, distorted the truth of the 13 years
following the first 12 years of my life. This was the age of my first
rape. The rapist had my mother's permission to do as he wished with
me. She was handsomely paid.

These traumatic experiences left me dysfunctional and paralyzed
by fear. I have hidden the truth of my past, conjuring up stories to
make myself look good in the eyes of others. Discussions about
mothers are always avoided, because I cannot be an enthusiastic
participant. I have no glowing, loving, caring pictures of my mother.
My portrait of her is dark, monstrous and menacing. Her arms do not
comfort. They hurt. Her lips have never kissed me. They spit in my
face. Her legs doesn't bring her to my side when I cry out in pain.
They kick me in my gut.

The pain of abuse seems like it happened yesterday, and the
shame of it causes me to keep my mouth closed. How can I talk, and
who can I tell these sordid details? Who can I tell that I have
experienced such unimaginable cruelties at the hands of my
protector?

A series of events, occurring during a six-week period, takes me
to a place where I'm suffocating. Daily my soul cries out for release,
and sleep eludes me at nights. Every fiber of my being screams,
begging for the shackles in which it has been imprisoned for so long,
to be broken.

Shame stops me from relating even a portion of my past to
anyone. I am afraid of being judged by my friends. I am scared that
the few people who say they love and respect me will stop caring
about me.

I do not want to be talked about behind my back. To be laughed at, scorned and ridiculed by a society that thinks a child is responsible for at least some of the injustices done to them. That's what my mother says even though she was the one who instigated the abuses against me.

This story has been told to no one. My former husband of 20 years has no inkling of my past. If he had even suspected the truth, he would have raced to a divorce lawyer putting distance between us as fast as possible, a long time ago. My present husband of two years is also in the dark. I'm trying to find the courage to enlighten him before production of this book is completed. I am in a boat, which is about to capsize. I need help finding wholeness in my life, and I hope this is a step in the right direction.

My friends – maybe they won't recognize my face on the cover. Maybe I won't tell them I have written a book. But that will not work. I talk too much.

O Lord, what are they going to think about me? I have concealed the truth of my past by telling them only about the few good things. The very person, who raped and abused me, is portrayed as the best part of my life. The details have been carefully erased.

But, if I can help even one person to break the insidious silence and shame of rape and abuse, then the snickers from the ignorant will be well taken.

My mother often tells me how she wished she had "pulled my tongue out from my head at birth, killing me." She pits us against one another, further alienating the family. Today we manage to be friends with one another. I thank God we survived.

I believe God was there and spoke to me the night I danced in a nightclub that was blue with cigarette smoke as I held a glass of whiskey in my hand. Four month later, He led me to attend a crusade, where He again spoke to me, overshadowing me with His Holy presence. He fought and won the battle with the devil for my soul.

As I embark on this journey, I can truly say that my healing is in progress. It is only by the grace of God that I have made it this far. There is hope, even when you think all is lost and life is hopeless.

Please send me your thoughts, questions, ideas, comments and suggestions. I will personally respond to each of you.

We may be contacted at:

www.revampmylifeministeries.com
Email: info.revampmylife@gmail.com
Twitter: revampmylife
Facebook: Marcia O'Connor

The names of the characters have been changed to protect the privacy of the persons depicted in this true story of my life.

Acknowledgements

My deepest and most sincere appreciation goes to God for His everlasting love and saving grace. It is only because He loves us so much, that He gave His life to save the human race, making it possible for sinners like me to have a place in His kingdom.

I am grateful to my supportive and loving family, who has encouraged me in the painful and tedious task of completing this work. It has been a long journey, paved with many tears and misgivings, but here I am, a survivor.

Mother; I have forgiven you for all the injustices you sanctioned and performed against me. You are lying silent in your grave. How I wish for one more opportunity to try and make things right between us.

May God bless you, and I pray that you'll be a part of the first resurrection.

Table of Contents

Chapter One

I WANT WHAT YOU HAVE

I am in bed, where I have been tossing around for hours. I pull the sheet up to my chest, and in a few minutes it's pushed aside again, kicked down to my ankles. The soles of my feet are cold, my hands are cold, my heart is breaking, my head is pounding. Sleep will elude me tonight, as it has done for too many nights before.

The pillows are punched, repositioned, turned over, tossed aside, and pulled back under my head again. Both sides are wet with my tears.

A new day is about to dawn. I get out of bed and walk to the window. The sight that meet my eyes causes a gasp of wonder to escape my lips. It's beautiful, the sun is shining on icicles hanging from the trees. It's a winter wonderland, snow is piled all the way up to the tops of the cars, covering them from my sight. I watch the children as they run out of their houses clad from head to toe in winter coats, gloves, mittens, ear muffs and boots. How on earth can they play in this snow? It is so cold.

I watch the world going by from my vantage point of the bedroom window, still trying to figure out how people are able to walk in what seems to be such slippery cold stuff. How will I get warm again? Am I going to be able to exist in this place? Where am I going to get warm clothes? Is this a mistake? Should I have come here to Canada, or should I have remained where I was, fighting my battles on the battleground of Kingston, Jamaica.

I Want What You Have

My old memories have kept me prisoner in the same old place, the place of regret and remorse, the place of pain and loss, the place of darkness and hopelessness. I want to get out of here, longing to have peace and hope in my heart. I search my soul for a flicker of something, a promise made to me, a desire waiting to be satisfied, a dream begging to be fulfilled.

The cold fingers of loneliness, regret and despair have a firm grip on my heart. I am desperate for a solution to my problems, but it all seems so dark and dismal. My mind is locked in its usual place, I can't stop thinking about my life, my painful life. The memories keep coming, my mind is reeling, the tears keep falling, I need a job, I need money, I need release, I must get help. That is why I am in this cold foreign land, I have come to find help, to establish a new life, to fight for a future. The only help I have right now is allowing the memories to flow. They flow freely through my head, breaking my heart all over again. O God, I am tired of crying. I miss my children.

I must find release before I explode.

A young mother of six has been widowed far too early, and the family has been plunged into abject poverty. Nothing had prepared them for this turn of events, there is no one for them to turn to for help, no sympathetic shoulders on which to cry. What are they going to do?

The sudden and untimely death of Billy Starky has wreaked havoc on Vira, his wife. She doesn't know what to do, she has no means of providing for her children, she needs help now if the family is to survive.

Vira cries out to God for help. "Lord, please help me."

On a whim, she packs up the few belongings that the family possesses, and they begin walking to another part of the parish. There has to be a better way. There has to be a better life – there just has to be. She doesn't know what the future holds for her and her children, but deep down in her heart, hope springs alive. Hope burns within her soul, giving her the tenancy to keep going, to keep forging ahead.

She wants to lie down and rest, maybe even join her husband in death, but she can be offered no such luxuries. She has six children to provide for.

A man who lives with his common-law wife in the community begins making frequent visits to the home. Soon his visits turn into overnight rendezvous within the leaky tar-and-shackle walls of the overcrowded home, which already houses a mother and six children. With another person, there is not enough space for another body to turn. When he spends the night, all six children sleep under the table. A sheet is used as a make-shift door, separating the adults from impressionable children.

Austin McLaren is a handsome man who had relocated from St. Catherine, another parish on the Island. It's rumored that he has fled St. Catherine to avoid supporting the six children he fathered there.

With the new relationship in full swing Vira is smiling again, there is a spark of hope for the future.

In small communities gossip travels fast, and before long the woman with whom Austin lives becomes privy to the fact he has formed another relationship. She is not happy. What is she going to do if the unthinkable happens? What if he leaves her for another woman, and not just another woman, but one who has six children of her own? What is he thinking? Has he forgotten that he fled the responsibilities of his own six children? Why on earth would he saddle himself with a brood of snotty-nosed, fatherless, children? She is not going to allow this to happen. She will, at any cost, protect their relationship.

Both women are in need of a man. Both of them want this man. Austin is definitely fresh blood, and he is probably one of the few unmarried men around. Both women are willing to fight for what they want. They have several confrontations in the streets, in the market, wherever their paths cross. In the meantime Austin enjoys the meals and comforts of both women.

On one of his visits to Vira, he tries to contribute to the household finances. With one of his charming smiles, he sticks his hand in his pocket, pulls it out and hand her some money. With a smile on her face Vira stretches out her hand to receive the badly needed funds. The smile freezes on her face as she looks at what he has placed in her palm. To her astonishment, there lies a shining coin worth a whopping 25 pennies. She is furious.

Slowly raising her eyes from her hand, she shoots daggers at him. Screaming, "What do you take me for? What am I supposed to do with this? Do you think this pittance can feed you for a week?"

The smile slowly ebbs from his face, replaced with embarrassment. "Ah …I'm sorry I thought it was enough. I'm just trying to help you out knowing that things are hard.

Lifting her left arm high over her head, she throws the coin as far away as she can. Then she spins around on her heels and walks into her home, slamming the door in his face.

Austin is not a rich man, but that is not the issue, he is a man, and is therefore worth fighting over. And fight they do. Vira decides that she was not willing to share him. She wants him to be a father to her fatherless children. After he stayed away from her for two days, she decides the time has come for her to claim what belongs to her. Marching to his home, she pounds on the door demanding he comes out to her. The other woman emerges, ordering her off her property. Vira has no intentions of leaving without what she has come to collect. She wants Mr. McLaren, and is here to issue the last notice to his woman to leave him alone. The other woman has the same intention, to keep what is hers. This dispute can only be settled one way.

A heavyweight championship fight is brewing. The prize: a man. And not just any man – this is a battle for the only eligible bachelor for miles around. He is willing to become father to her six children, and she is a woman who desperately needs a provider. Like a lioness protecting her cubs, she rises to the challenge. Vira's words hold a warning.

"I am warning you, leave him alone. He is mine now. You are not woman enough to keep your man at home, so he came to me. Keep your dirty, filthy hands off him. If you don't leave him alone you will be sorry."

"He is mine. We have been together for over one year and were happy until you showed up. You are going to leave him alone if it means that I have to beat you."

They fight. What a sight: two grown women getting into a fistfight over a man. Like the cats they are, blows fly through the air, hitting and scratching, yelling and cussing at each other. They pull hair and clothes and fight some more. When the dust settled only the winner is left standing.

Vira has literally torn the clothes off the other woman's back, leaving her desperately trying to cover her nakedness with the pieces of rags hanging from her shoulders. The neighbors stand by watching this drama unfold. Her children have barely been able to hold their heads up, but now the ground holds special interest as they walk around. It has been bad enough being labeled the poorest in the district. Now they have another stigma attached to them.

Where is Austin during all of this? What does he have to say about which woman he loves and whom he wants to be with? He is given no choice in the matter. When he returns from work at the end of the day, Vira tells him that he now belongs to her and is never to be seen with the other woman again. His pleadings fall on deaf ears; he is not even allowed to return to his former home to collect his belongings. She strides over to the house demanding his clothing. They are thrown out the door. Vira proudly picks up each piece, tucking them under her arms, hearing the snickers behind her as she walks away. At home she hangs them over the only chair in the house.

Vira controls every aspect of Austin's life. Money is very important to her, and to his embarrassment, she begin showing up at his place of employment on Friday afternoons, going directly to the foreman of the carpenter shop to collect his pay. If he is lucky, he will be given one pound every two weeks for his personal use. If at anytime she feels the need for additional funds, he has to give it up, or give her a good reason why it had been spent. He has no idea what he had gotten himself into. If he thought life with his six children was hard, the noose around his neck has now been tightened one-hundred fold, leaving just enough room for his finger to wiggle around, relieving the pressure from his Adam's apple.

Eventually, the embarrassment becomes too much for the beaten woman to bear. Vira has gone out of her way to flaunt her victory in her face. The district is too small for two lionesses to reign, so the beaten woman pack up her belongings and moves out of the area. The residents ostracizes Vira because they do not agree with her actions. She doesn't care. She has forgotten their kindness to her and her children. Now with a man to call her own, she no longer needs them.

Soon she is fighting with Austin. During a loud verbal fight, Vira grabs a machete and with precision, chops him squarely in his forehead. He reels from the shock of the blow, falling backward, as blood spouts from the open wound, blinding his eye. He stumbles into the bushes, yelling for help. "Lawd, I'm dead now! Help! Somebody help me! My eye, Lawd! I can't see. Help!"

No help comes from Vira or from anyone else. He wails like a wounded animal dashing through the bushes, trying to find relief from the pain in his face. Back and forth he runs, begging for help. With arms folded across her chest Vira remain aloof to his suffering, closing her ears against his wailing. Desperately he tries to save his sight protecting it with his hand. Hours later he emerges, bloody and crazed with pain. The children huddle together crying at the awful sight they have witnessed. Vira tells them to shut up, or they will also receive a beating. Then she walks away, ignoring Austin's cries. The girls do their best to clean the wound.

To everyone's surprise, the wound heals and his eye is not lost, but he will go to his grave wearing his scar like a badge of honor.

Chapter Two

ALLIANCE WITH THE DEVIL

It's a balmy Thursday evening in St. Thomas, Jamaica. At about 6:30 pm, on August 1, 1957, in the Morant Bay hospital, a beautiful baby girl makes her entrance into the world. She is the daughter of Vira Starcky and Austin McLaren. She weighs in at a whopping 10 pounds, breaking the hospital's scale as she is placed on it. She opens her mouth letting out her first cry. Her mother takes an instant dislike to her, but her father falls in love.

After weeks of disagreement about the naming of his precious baby. Austin wants to name his daughter Catherine. Vira wins the argument and she is named Marcia Elaine, the first child of their union.

My older siblings tell me of my mother's constant beatings of me, and my father's attempts at defending me. They also tell me how they carried me around on their hips, even when I was old enough to walk. One of my sisters claims that her hip has been permanently misaligned from carrying me on it. "Why did you do that?" I ask. "Because your father loved you so much he didn't want you to walk on the dirt."

Am I responsible for those decisions? Maybe Mama blames me for the life they created. The noose around her neck must have gotten a bit tighter with the appearance of another child. Life could not have promised much hope for a poor woman who has now given birth to 11 children, with seven to care for. Frustration and anger must have been her constant companions as she trudged through her daily toils.

And so my mother despises me and my father adores me. He tries his best to protect me from unnecessary whippings, but he has to work. The family has to be provided for, and so like all the other children, I am at my mother's mercy.

We continue living in St. Thomas, but the address changes to a larger place, more accommodating for the growing family. While Daddy works, Vira never stop looking for ways to improve the lot of her little flock. Even in her harsh treatment of us, a tiny thread to make us better runs deep within her. In her inability to provide for us, she turns to others. Help has a strange way of coming with a price tag; at times the price listed on the tag far exceeds the value. One price, which should never be paid by anyone, is the sacrifice of children for a few dollars or a bag of food. Unfortunately, that became our legacy.

Mama forms a friendship with a man who demands payment in the highest and most reprehensible form. Her daughters. As the years pass, we are taken to the altar one by one, and offered up as sacrifices to the devil clad in a suit, sitting in a big house on the hill, serving his country from one of the highest positions in the land.

How Mama met and formed an alliance with the most powerful man in the parish of St. Thomas remains a mystery. Vira Starcky, and the mayor, who ran for political office and was elected as the government representative for the parish, are best friends. The alliance is so strong that he is named as my godfather.

Two years after my birth, Bridget Pansy is born into the family. She is followed by Alicia Janice, who is followed by Cheryl Anita. Gregory Anthon Alistair is the last of the bunch of children. Vira began giving birth at the age of 16. The first surviving child, Amelia, was born to her at the age of 19. The last child, Gregory, at the age of 41. Is it any wonder that mother is angry and bitter, after 25 years of baby production? Even the finest machine comes to a screeching halt from its constant usage and production.

Her children have not escaped the wrath of a woman who apparently had never known the love of her mother and had no time to love herself. Nor had she formed any type of lasting friendships with neighbors or friends. She has never experienced the life-changing love of Jesus, although she regularly attends church and is very strict in the traditions of her beliefs.

At the time of my birth, Amelia, the eldest child was 14 years old and had already left home. She could no longer withstand the physical, and emotional abuse, and decided to make it on her own. What could happen to her out there that had not happened at home?

Victoria soon follows Amelia, leaving home looking for a better life. As time passes, the other children have been given away to other families who continue the abuse. Lester and Leroy had been given to a carpenter who promised to teach them the business. Lynnette is given to a teacher who carries on the emotional abuse of her mother, scarring her for life. Patricia, who is two years my senior, remains at home.

My first memory of home is at about five years old. Bridget and I have contracted whooping cough. Locked in the house, forbidden to play outside, we pass our time between bouts of coughing, and looking out the window at the others playing in the warm sunshine. On the third day of our isolation, we notice our father returning home, carrying an animal by its tail. We almost fall out the window, as we lean forward to see what strange creature he carries. Mama sees him coming, and rushes out to inquire. Stopping in her tracks she yells, "What are you doing with that filthy field rat?"

"I'm going to make rat soup for the girls; a woman in the market told me that it's the cure for whooping cough."

"You must be mad," mother retorted. "Take that dirty thing out of my yard."

Daddy persists. "Do you prefer that they die? Don't you hear how bad they sound, especially at nights?"

Holding up the bunch of bushes in her hand she explains, "I am going to boil them some bush tea. Let the dirty rat go. Are you crazy?"

"But this will work faster than any bush tea. Everybody in the market tells me that that's what they give to their children when they have whooping cough."

Getting angrier by the minute, she explodes. "Man, get that filthy thing out of my yard! And you had better not let it go here so it can come into the house. Over my dead body are you going to make rat soup in this house. Get out of here you stupid man."

Dejected, Daddy returns to the field; where he disposes of the rat. That was one occasion, (maybe the only one), for which we are glad Mama stood up to Daddy.

Country life can be peaceful, times can be hard and people may be poor. Usually, there are no modern amenities. But life is simple. Expenses are the bare minimum because food is grown in the fields or in the backyard. Animals are raised and used for the feeding of the family, and children are supposed to be free to run and play, growing up strong and healthy. Illiteracy is high, and tempers flare quickly. Families are large, because in most cases, as soon as a woman weans a baby, she conceives again.

My family of 11 children is large, but not unique. The blending of families is quite common, because men are likely to die at an early age, either due to accidents or the unavailability of immediate medical care. The difference between my family and others is the open hostility my mother displays towards us. She has given birth to 15 children, 11 of whom have survived. After her losses, one may think that she might have thanked God for each child that is born healthy and survived infancy. Instead, she grows more resentful toward each one, almost to the point of blaming the children for their existence.

Mama constantly tells me how she wished she had "pulled my tongue out at birth and killed me." I live in constant fear of this threat being carried out. To make it harder for her, I held my tongue firmly between the shackles of my teeth.

Up to my age of seven, we lived in St. Thomas. One day my parents pack up our belongings, load them in a truck, help us up into the truck, and tell us to go to sleep. We are moving. The truck rolls out onto the dirt road, leaving our little home behind. "Where are we going?" we quietly ask one another, wide-eyed with fear and excitement. Mama hears us and chimes in, "Go to sleep the lot of you, we are moving to Kingston, that's the big city. When you wake up in the morning we'll be there. Now I don't want to have to talk to any of you again, close your eyes and go to sleep."

We valiantly try to be quiet as we watch the countryside pass by. We want to see everything, but it's a long trip and it's dark outside. Soon, one by one, our eyelids droop, and we are off to sleep, dreaming of life in the big city. My dreams are filled with fun and adventure. We are moving to the city.

The next day, tired but excited, we arrive. Our parents unpack our belongings and we explore the new surroundings. Everything looks different. Instead of bushes and dirt roads we see buildings and paved streets. The bathroom and kitchen are located inside the house. It's a big house, the biggest we had ever seen. Our eyes pop out when we see all the bedrooms. All three of them. Instantly we fall in love with our new home at number 3 Paradise Street, Kingston, Jamaica.

Across the street from our new home is a huge building surrounded by wire fence. "What is that?" I ask Daddy. That is the Mental Health Sanitarium, called Belleview Asylum. In other words, it's a madhouse where the mad people are kept so that they are not roaming the streets," he replies. At one end of the street is the ocean. "O my goodness," I cry, "We are in heaven." Life takes on a new meaning. We are happy with the new-found freedom. Daddy gets hired as the carpenter at the Children's Hospital, and my siblings and I begin attending school.

On Sunday mornings Daddy takes all of us down to the beach for a swim. We frolic in the warm waters and build sand castles, while soaking up the radiant sunshine. We return home to hot Johnnycakes with ackee and salt fish, washed down with hot chocolate tea. After breakfast, we run outside to play. For pennies, we buy balls sold over the high walls of the asylum. We throw our pennies over the wall and the balls are tossed to us. We hear voices belonging to faces we saw peering through the holes as they peddled their wares from their place of confinement.

One Sunday evening, while playing in our huge back yard with a newly purchased ball , I notice that the cords have begun to unravel. As it comes apart in my hand I am fascinated to discover the inward makings of the ball. The last bit of string falls away, revealing tightly rolled newspaper. From this wad an unpleasant odor assails my nostrils. What's on the inside? Gingerly I rip into the newspaper. Before long I am looking at the core of the ball. A load of human waste. Screaming I toss the vile object as far away as I can. My screams bring Daddy outside. I tell him of my discovery. He chuckles. "What do you expect? You bought it from madmen in an asylum." There ended our patronage of the wares over the wall.

The family begins attending church on a regular basis. Mama's first husband, Billy, was a member of the Seventh-day Adventist Church. (SDA). She had learned about the denomination through him, and had experienced kindness from members of the faith after his death. When she traveled to St. Thomas, the SDA church had offered help to her family. Mama had never forgotten how generous they had been to her and her children and although never baptized she considers herself a member of the faith. Daddy, on the other hand had never heard of the SDA church. He had grown up in the Anglican faith worshipping on Sunday. Of course this caused great conflict, but mother won. The household attends church on Saturday. Mama and Daddy have been in a relationship for ten years, and have five children together. The church frowns upon the common-law household. To become members of this religious sect, my parents need to get married.

On June 8, 1966, a beautiful Sunday evening, my parents exchanged wedding vows in the North Street Seventh-day Adventist Church. Mama is ecstatic; she looks radiant in a calf-length white bridal dress. A shoulder-length veil covers her head, and she carries a bunch of delightful white flowers. Daddy is stunningly handsome in a cream suit. The children are all decked out in finery, and fearing the beating we have been warned will be forthcoming for any misbehavior, we display perfect manners. The reception following the ceremony is a fun affair. The church outdid itself, providing, food, drink and a very enjoyable and memorable day.

One week later, both parents are baptized in the same church. Everyone rejoices. The entire family are now official members of the Seventh-day Adventist denomination.

I am a student at the Windward Road Primary School, and loving every moment of it. Walking to school with my little sisters each morning, getting there late all sweaty and tired is only the beginning of my days. Recess is time spent on the playfield playing catch, dandy shandy, baseball, and any game an empty orange juice box, or the remains of an orange can be used to play.

14

The large tamarind tree in the front of the school yard provides a good hiding place at lunch time when I try to hide my greasy paper-bag lunch. The oil from the fried dumplings and salt-fish fritters have seeped through, telling on me that my lunch was cooked and brought from home, instead of being prepared on the premises.

Who wants to eat school lunch anyway, affectionately called "bullo slush," when you can have your mother's fried salt-fish fritters, washed down with a bottle of "sugar and water?" I eat quickly, trying to get finished before my classmates discover me eating from the greasy paper bag.

It's Friday afternoon and the last bell rings, and in an orderly line, we march out of the classroom. But instead of hitting the streets, pounding the pavement on the return trip home, the children head for the cafeteria. There we stand in line, waiting our turn to receive a packed paper bag.

There is no shame in carrying these bags: they are filled with goodies to be carried home to our parents. Inside my shopping bag are smaller bags filled with milk powder, corn meal, flour and rice. I hurry out the gate, hoping that the girl to whom told the four letter curse word in class will not notice me and douse me over my head with her milk powder. The teacher had called me to the front of the class, made me openly apologize to her, and then I had been taken to the bathroom where my mouth was washed out with soap and water. But she had threatened to get back at me. I must hurry away from the school yard – walking home covered with white milk powder from head to foot cannot be fun.

Mama is glad to receive the bag of goodies and I am rewarded with a handful of milk powder in which I immediately stick my tongue. So sweet and sticky, I can't get enough of this stuff. When Mama isn't looking I sneak a few more handfuls, trying not to choke as I lick my hand clean. The rumblings of my stomach and my frequent bathroom visits that night tell on me.

It's nurse week at school" the Ministry of Health has sent nurses into the school to examine the students, making sure that all vaccinations in the prevention of childhood diseases have been received. It's my turn, and the sight of the needle causes my stomach to drop to my feet and my knees to go weak. Regardless of my inward turmoil, the needle is stabbed into my shoulder as I scream in pain.

My mother takes me to the dentist because I have been complaining about a toothache for weeks. It's my first visit to a dentist, and I am scared. He tells me to open wide, then he pokes around in my mouth. The decayed molar has to be taken out immediately. He gets what looks to me like pliers, tells me again to open wide, inserts the instrument into my mouth, fastens it around my tooth, and begin pulling on the tooth.

I begin screaming bloody murder. Mama tells me to behave, and the dentist tells me to be still, as a nurse holds me down in the chair. I feel as if I am going to die. He gives a big pull, I give a big scream. I wake up on the couch with my mother sitting next to me, fanning me with a newspaper. The pain in my mouth is horrible, my tongue finds the spot where my tooth used to be, and instead I find a cotton ball stuffed into the empty tooth socket. I begin crying again. My mouth hurts.

We are constantly on the move, either because of problems with the neighbors (my mother lives peacefully with no one), or because the neighborhood wakes up to find a neighbor hanging from a mango tree in the front yard. My parents do not think about the importance of maintaining some type of stability or even accessibility for their children's education. Getting to school becomes more of a problem. I have to take the city bus, and get myself there on time. One morning, Mama tells me that she has no money to give me for my bus fare. I get dressed for school and try walking to school, but abandon the idea and return home crying, because my eight-year-old brain cannot remember the bus route. I have learned not to form friendships, remaining aloof from my counterparts and peers. This way no one will ask me why I missed school.

Soon, after taking up residence in yet another new home on Mountain View Avenue, Daddy sits us down and tells us that we have six older brothers and sisters. He explains that they have a different mother than we do, and that two of his other children want to meet his new family. Mama, of course is furious, but Daddy is determined not to allow her to bully him into abandoning his children again.

Two weeks later, Daddy comes home with a tall young man proudly dressed in the uniform of a police officer.

"This is your brother Ethan."

I had never met a policeman before and am in awe of him. He extends his hand to me and I walk towards him. "Hello, I am Ethan. Pleased to meet you."

"Hello, I am Marcia. Pleased to meet you, too." My sisters follow my lead, each one introducing herself to our new brother. Mama sits down with him, and soon she is inviting him to stay for dinner. By the end of the afternoon I am in love with him, and after his departure, my sisters and I reminisce about how awesome our policeman big brother is. He comes by often, and each visit is delightful as he entertains us with stories of escapades and encounters with bad guys.

A few years after meeting Ethan, he tells us that he is getting married. Bridget and I will be flower girls in his wedding. On the chosen Sunday afternoon, we stand next to our brother and Greta as they take their vows, smiling proudly for the camera in our yellow dresses and a-size-too-large white shoes. After the birth of their daughter, Sasha, Greta becomes ill, and she stays in our home while she recuperates.

There is an odd smell in the house, and Mama is in a flurry of activities, she is cleaning everywhere with Dettol and is shooing us out of the living room to go outside and play. I want to know what is going on, so I sit down on the couch to listen to the argument between Mama and Greta. I don't understand what they are talking about – something about cheating and getting syphilis. Mama notices me on the couch and yells at me to go outside. I linger in the doorway, still listening and watching the drama as it unfolds. Greta gets off the couch where she had been sitting, and Mama instantly uses the Dettol-soaked rag to wipe it down. Then she spreads a sheet of newspaper over it. She sees me standing in the doorway and gives me instructions, "Marcia I want you and the other children to make sure that you spread newspaper on the couch and on all the chairs before you sit down."

"Why do we have to sit on newspaper?"

"Because Greta has syphilis and I don't want you children to catch it."

"What is syphilis and how can we catch it?"

"Don't ask me any questions. Just do as I say. Now go outside and stop listening to big-people conversation."

I believe that before the word dysfunctional was coined, my family suited the meaning to perfection. There is no real stability in my life. I live in constant fear of my mother: her heavy left hand has no mercy. It only metes out punishment. It is never open to a hurt, crying child to run for refuge. Actually, the wielding of those arms has hurt the crying child. We have no contact or relationship with grandparents, aunts or other family members. We are allowed to speak with no one outside the home; no friends from school or neighbors visit the home. We are strictly commanded to keep no friends at school, no playing after school or idling about. Her philosophy is this: "There are enough of you to keep each other company. You don't need friends."

The only friends we have are those introduced into the family by mother. A man known to us as Blue Bird is brought into our home as a friend of the family. He is allowed to visit often and plays with us in the yard under the big mango tree. He pushes us high in the air on the swing, and squeals of laughter come from us. When no one is looking, he runs his hand up my leg, touching private places.

I'm sitting on the swing under the mango tree, holding my crying baby brother in my arms. Without intending to, I fall asleep. The sound of an object hitting the ground, followed by a loud cry, awakens me. Mama comes rushing out of the house to find me trying to pick up and comfort the fallen child. I am beaten with a branch from the mango tree, and sent to bed without dinner.

The children at school are all talking about their new television sets. With mouth wide open, I listen to the stories of the shows they have been watching, asking questions about where the people are hiding as they are being watched on the screen? Or where do they go when the set is turned off? No one has an answer for me. I want a television set so I can look for the people.

"Daddy, I am going to get an 'O' on my test at school and fail my exam." With a frown on my father's brow, he asks, "Why are you going to fail your test?" "Because our teacher told us to watch the news and listen to what the people are talking about so we can know what is going on in the world, then she is going to give us a test on it.

18

She says that there is a lot going on right here on the Island and we need to be able to discuss the current events in social studies class. Then she is going to test us to see how much we remember."

Daddy asks, "Did she really say that? How can she expect you children to know what is going on here much less in another country?"

"All the other children in my class have a television set at their house, I am the only one who don't have one, so I am the only one who is going to fail the test," I reply.

"I am sure you are not the only one who doesn't have a television at home. People don't have money to buy these things, but I will see what I can do to get you children a set for you to watch."

Daddy purchases a brand new black-and-white, one-channel Sylvania television. No longer do we have to peek over the fence, straining our necks to watch the neighbors' set, or have someone close the door in our faces when they see us trying to get a glimpse of *Romper Room* or *Sesame Street* from their television set. I proudly announce to my classmates that I have a television set in my home, and I can join in the conversation about our favorite television program.

It's a somber Sunday afternoon on the Island. One of our dignitaries has died, and today is his funeral. Silently we watch the procession on our own television. At the end of the ceremony, our parents release us to go outside and play. I dash out the door into the back yard, heading for the swing. A sharp pain in my foot stops me in my tracks. Dropping to the ground I turn my foot bottom up, and there, imbedded in my flesh, is a rusty, six-inch nail. Daddy comes out to see what all the noise is about, and falls to his knees at my side. He tells mother to bring him a wet cloth, using it to apply pressure to the area, he pulls the nail out of my foot.

Pain shoots up to my ankle, as Daddy picks me up. We hobble across the street to the bus stop, where I sit on a bench, waiting for a bus to take us to the hospital. In the emergency room I am given a tetanus shot, and told to stay off my feet. A series of shots needs to be administered to avoid infection, or worst yet, the loss of my foot. This is repeated for several weeks, until I am pronounced healed.

I like living at this home on Mountain View Avenue. I immensely enjoy the large back yard, the mango tree, the swing and the long verandah. Its larger than the other homes we have lived in.

One of my chores is to iron the school uniforms of my younger sisters. One Sunday afternoon as I am laboring over the ironing board, a young girl from the front house joins me on the verandah. She tells me that her mother, who lives in the United States of America, will be arriving in a few days to take her back with her to live in the USA. She pulls a penny from her pocket and places it on the ironing board, daring me to put the iron down on it to see how hot it will get. I take the dare, and go a step further with the red-hot penny. Picking up the hot coin with a clothes hanger, I drop it on the girl's leg.

She squeals in pain, jumping up from her seat, knocking the coin onto the floor. Mama comes running. When she sees what I have done, she takes the girl inside the house, applying a cold rag and ointment to the red swollen round area. "What am I going to tell her parents? Her mother will be here in two days to take her to America. What have you done, you stupid child?"

I get a beating.

We move again, and this time we are living in a house that is too small for the family. Getting to school is an even bigger problem, but I get on the city bus each morning, figuring out where the transfer is made, arriving on time. I am determined to get an education, even if I have to take three buses to get to primary school.

There is some type of occupancy restriction for the house we live in, and we are over the limit, and we have to take turns playing outside. The neighbors cannot know how many of us live here. It's funny at first, but soon we begin feeling like prisoners. Tempers flair easily, and the belt rains down on us just as frequently. One day the landlord comes by unexpectedly, and too many of us are outside playing. She discovers six faces peering at her as she asks for our mother.

"Mama a woman is at the door asking for you."

"Mrs. McLaren are all these children yours?"

"Yes. All of them are mine."

"When you rented the house I asked you how many children you had and you said three. Now how many do I see: six or seven?"

Not missing a beat, Mama replied, "You tell me, who is going to rent me a house with six children? What does it matter to you how many of us live in here as long as you get your rent on time? As a matter of fact it's not the first of the month, and the rent isn't due yet.

So what are you doing here? You are trespassing on my property. I suggest you leave before I call the police."

Mama slams the door in her face, signaling the end of the conversation.

The only bathroom in the two-room apartment is located upstairs. Two of us sleep on a bed under the stairs. It's summer break from school, and we are all stuck in the house. The toilet is used and flushed many times each day.

One Friday afternoon while both parents are out of the home, someone flushes the toilet. Instead of the contents smoothly disappearing the bowl fills up with water. The child yells for me to come here now. Running up the stairs I meet water and feces pouring down the stairs. Bridget and I clean up the mess, then we turn our attention to the soaked mattress under the stairs. Pulling it along, walking backwards into the yard, excruciating pain suddenly shoots through my foot. Screaming, I drop the mattress and grab my foot. To my horror, my big toe is almost severed. My screams bring the neighbor running to investigate. Seeing the bloody toe hanging by skin, she quickly ties my foot with a towel, stemming the blood flow.

Daddy comes home and takes me to the hospital where shots, stitches and weeks of hobbling along slowly bring about my healing. The toilet continues overflowing. It becomes as much a way of life as running to the ice truck to get bits of ice chips to cool our thirst.

I am ten years old, and have a huge protrusion on my stomach, I look at the stomachs of my sisters, none of them have what I have.

"Mama what is this?"

"You have a big navel."

"How come I am the only one who has it?"

"Because you have a weak stomach or something."

"The children at school are teasing me because they can see it through my uniform, they call me elephant trunk and other names."

"Alright I'll talk to your father and see if he can make the arrangements at the hospital to have it removed."

I am happy, now that my elephant trunk is going to be removed.

Before long I am taken to the hospital and doctors are looking at my big navel, talking about the surgery to remove it.

One morning my parents take me to the hospital again, telling me this time I am going to be admitted to have my big navel removed. Daddy is with me as I am changed into a hospital gown and told to get up into the hospital bed.

He sits down at my bedside and explains, "You are going to have surgery to fix this problem tomorrow morning. When you wake up from the surgery, your big navel will be gone and your stomach will look like your sisters. See this gown you are wearing? This is a good one because it goes on over your head, but if they put one on you that is open in the back, it's because that had to cut it off a dead child. Tell them to take it off and put one like this one you."

"Okay, Daddy," I reply.

"You are going to be here in the hospital for a few nights. Be a brave girl. I will come and see you in the morning when I come to work."

"Okay, Daddy."

"Alright, I have to go now. Have a good night. See you in the morning."

"Good night, Daddy."

I watch my Daddy walk away from me. Feeling the tears sting my eyes. I close them to keep them the tears from spilling out. Someone is calling my name. I open my eyes and a nurse is standing over me.

"Good morning, Marcia. How are you today?"

"I am fine."

"Good. We will be taking you down to operating theater for surgery now. I want you to scoot over from your bed on to this one so we can roll you down. Can you do that?"

"Yes I can."

I move from one bed to the other, and a sheet is pulled over me. I am being rolled down the halls to the room the nurse had called the theatre. There, I am moved onto another bed. Big lights are hanging down from the ceiling, doctors and nurses are wearing masks covering their mouths and noses, and their hands are in gloves. I am wondering if they are all sick. A nurse tells me that she is going to put the mask she is holding over my nose, and I should count from one to ten.

"One, two, three, four, five, six...."

When I awake, I am back in my room, and my parents are looking down at me. "Are you alright?" Mama asks.

Nodding my head, I move my hand to my stomach. Its covered with bandages and it hurts, but it's flat. My big navel is gone. No more elephant-trunk name calling.

That night I am changed into a gown that opens in the front. I don't know what to do. Should I tell the nurse to take it off me? She walks away from my bed, and I am afraid to speak my fears. I drift off to sleep, a very interrupted sleep as dreams of ghosts and goblins, hands of dead children trying to take their gown off my back. I wake up sweating – no more sleep for me tonight, in this gown that belongs to someone else.

My parents become aware of a new subdivision being built by the government. A number of the homes will be allocated to families who qualify under a housing program. Mama immediately contacts her influential government friend, my godfather. With his help, coupled with Daddy's position at the hospital, we become eligible for one of the new homes.

It's August, in the year 1969. It's an exciting time. Something is about to happen: we are going to move. The move itself isn't exciting: I have moved more times than I can remember in my five years since we moved to the city. What is exciting is that this will be our last move. We are moving to our own brand new home in Duhaney Park, Kingston 20. The new house has two bedrooms and one bathroom, but I am oblivious to the cramped space. It's the first place I have to call my own. No more hiding from landlords, or having to move to another home because the neighbors dislike Mama. Even if they don't get along, she will have to stick it out. This is our home.

Windward Road Primary School is now a place of the past. It's impossible to travel the distance twice daily, so I am enrolled in Pembroke Hall Primary School. When school opens in September, 1967, I will be a new student in grade 8. It's time for me to study for and sit the Common Entrance Examination, and it is critical that I pass this exam. It's the only way to gain entry into a high school, since there are no funds to pay my way through a private high school.

I beg my parents to allow me to remain at school after classes and take private lessons, which will prepare me to sit and pass this important exam. Mama turns me down. "I have no money to pay for private lessons for you, I don't see why you need to take extra lessons to take a test, the teachers should teach you what you need to learn in school."

"But Mama, the teacher says that since I just came to the school I need extra lessons and this is my only chance to take the exam since I didn't take it at Windward Road. I won't be able to go to high school if I don't take and pass the Common Entrance Exam."

"Gal, get out of my sight. Who do you think you are talking to me about paying precious money for you to take some test to go to high school? None of your older sisters or brothers went to any high school and they are doing just fine. As a matter of fact, you are not going to take any test to go any place. If you want to be all high and mighty, then go to the secondary school which is next door to where you go now, I have no money to waste on you."

"But Mama, I just want to take the exam, I argue, "If I pass you don't have to pay…."

Smack to my face. "Shut your mouth and don't back talk me. See what I am talking about? You already don't have any manners! You want to come and lord it over me in this house about going to high school. Go sit down, and I don't want to hear one more word about private lessons or any high school."

Mother's hatred for me grows as I evolve from a girl into a teenager. Unlike other parents, who proudly smile as their children grow up, she denounces and curses me, making me ashamed of my budding body. Instead of thanking God that despite all the hardships she has endured, her children have escaped involvement in drugs or alcohol, or running with the wrong crowd, and she threatens to kill me. Her threats to pour hot oil down my ears while I sleep are so real that I live in fear of going to sleep. At nights I try to stay awake to watch over my sisters. Inevitably sleep takes over, but not before I hold a pillow tightly over my head.

Physical abuse is one thing, but mental and emotional abuse is an insidious evil. At the hands of my mother, I suffer both physical and mental abuse. For as long as I can remember, outside the hearing of my father, I am told over and over again, that I am less than nothing.

"You Mr. Mac pickneys were never wanted. The entire lot of you can go to hell for all I care. Billy is the only husband I ever had. He is the only man I ever loved. Amelia is the only child I ever had and all the rest of you are nothing but garbage. I hate the whole lot of you."

I hang my head in shame.

After giving me a particularly vicious beating, she makes me look in her eyes as she tells me how much she hates me.

"I wish I had pulled your tongue out of your head when you were born and killed you. I hate the sight of you! Get out of my sight, you piece of shit."

Then she spits in my face.

Spitting in my face is just another way for her to humiliate me. It is one of the lowest degrees of humiliation, and she has mastered the technique.

Bridget is unaware that she is committing a mortal sin by turning on the television without asking permission. Mother comes up behind her, and weilding a high-heeled shoe as a weapon, and chops Bridget in the head while screaming at her for touching her prized possession. In fright Bridget spins around, and is met with a wad of spit in her face. We look on in horror.

I yell, "Bridget, spit back in her face!"

"No, she is my mother," Bridget replies

While blood flows down her face, and stinking spit drips onto her blouse, we help Bridget outside, cleaning her up and comforting her. Bridget sports a hole in the side of her head where mother's stiletto heel lodged itself, barely missing her eye when mother threw it at her.

"I can kill any one or the entire bunch of you and get away with it because I have quicksilver in my head and will be diagnosed as crazy. No judge will lock me up in prison because I know all of them."

She is right. For some strange reason she knows and is friendly with the entire police force. They hold her in high esteem. Officers make frequent visits to the home. On one such visit, one officer remarks, "Oh, what a lovely lady you have for a mother, she reminds me of my mother. You children had better listen to your mother. She is a wise woman and will never steer you wrong."

If they only knew the hell that the children of the lovely lady live in. I have no idea what quicksilver in her head is, and I am trying my best not to find out.

The neighborhood children refer to Mama as an "obeah woman," further ostracizing us from society. She is feared by all, but not as much as by those of us living under the same roof with her. Daddy does not escape her wrath; he is berated and cursed every day of the week. At nights, I lie awake listening to them fight. After he gets dressed one morning, the sole of his feet began to itch. By the end of the day his feet are swollen to twice their size. He scratches his feet with everything his hands find. He turns his shoe over, knocking the bottom, to see if an insect had hidden itself in the toes, and white power flutters in the air. He swears she has worked obeah on him, trying to swell his body until it burst. We have no idea what to believe, each of us run for our shoes, turning them over to loosen whatever could be hidden therein. Shoes and clothing are worn with extreme caution.

After years of ferocious fighting between my parents, Daddy packs his bags and moves out of his house. Mama finds him and rains terror at the home of the friend who had taken him in. He moves back home. It's a classic case of, "I don't want you but I would rather see you dead than someone else have you."

One day Mama sends me to the corner shop with another note to be handed to the shopkeeper. I know that the note is asking for food on credit, and I also know that the shopkeeper is going to embarrass me by reading the note aloud and telling me to tell my mother that she cannot extend any more credit to her until the previous balance has been paid. She, along with two other shopkeepers, told me so yesterday.

I hang around outside the door, waiting for the perfect moment when the shop is empty to enter. Each time the last person walks out and I put my foot on the step, someone else enters, and I slink back into the shadows. Tired of playing the game of waiting for the perfect moment, I drag my feet back home with an answer on my lips which I know my mother is not going to like.

"Where is the stuff that I sent you to the shop to get?" she asks when she sees my empty hands.

"Mama, Miss Lisa says to tell you that she cannot credit you any more until you pay the bill."

"She says what? You go back to that shop and tell that woman that I want… You know what? Let me go talk to her myself."

"Oh God no, don't go Mama, I'll go back. What do you want me to tell her?"

"No, I will go, since you can't carry a message, and I have to do everything myself. I will go and beg the woman to credit me her food to feed you until my money come. Watch your little brother 'til I come back."

Watch, my little brother: she is going to kill me when she comes back.

"Marcia come here to me."

"Yes, Mama."

"Didn't I send you to the shop with a note for Miss Lisa?"

"Yes Mama."

"I just went to see the woman ready to tell her off, only to find out that you didn't give her the note at all. She said she saw you hanging around the door, but you never came in and gave her anything, then you come back here with a mouthful of lies. Come here to me."

"But Mama, I was..."

"You was what? When I send you out, I expect you to do exactly as I tell you. You don't decide what to do. You do as I tell you. Do you understand that?"

Wham goes the punch to my stomach, smack goes the slap to my face, thump is her left fist into my rib. The air rushes out of my lungs as I bend over at the waist in pain, my head is roughly pulled up by my hair. I open my eyes to look at her, and instantly close them in horror, just a fraction of a second too late – even my eyes stings with the wad of disgusting spit that splatters onto my face.

The beating continues, even as the spittle drips down my face into my mouth. I'm unable to wipe it away because my hands are busy protecting my budding breasts which are the target of her punches.

"Do you think you are a big woman in here, who when I send you out you decide what you don't want to do? Do you think that because you starting to grow breasts you are too big to do as I tell you?"

"No Mama."

Punch. "Shut up, I didn't ask you any question. Learn to do what I tell you to do."

I groan.

Wham to my breast.

27

"Get out of my sight, and since you are too big and too good to deliver a note asking for food on credit to feed the lot of you, you will not eat one rice grain of this dinner tonight."

As I turn to slink away, a swift kick into my back sends me flying into the couch. I crawl up the stairs, get into bed, remaining there for the remainder of the evening.

Patricia, whom I follow in birth order, is the oldest child in the home, and there is constant conflict between us. One Friday evening, she is cleaning the house, using Red Rexo floor polish and a coconut brush to polish and shine the terrazzo tiles. She calls me and sends me on an errand. "Go upstairs and bring me the book which is lying on the bed." I take a step forward and she yells at me, "Don't walk on the floor that I just cleaned." I check to see if I had grown wings, there is none attached to my back. "How do you expect me to go upstairs without walking on the floor? I can't fly." Getting in my face she explains. "I'm giving you to the count to ten to go get me my book. If you step on the floor and I see one mark I'm going to whip you. One, two, three... I step on the newly polished floor and she punches me, I take another step and she hits me again. Turning around I balled my fist and hit her soundly in the stomach. We fight. I get a sound beating, but that's all right, because she won't mess with me again. I get another whipping when mother returns home and hears the story.

Mother hates me, and I have no contact with my older siblings. Another part of Mother's insidious evil that she perpetrates against me is that she often tells me how her older children want nothing to do with me. What have I done to make my older sisters hate me?

Daddy cannot protect me from the reign of terror under which I live. He goes off to work daily, not knowing what craziness he will return to at the end of the day. At the slightest provocation, or if Mother gets upset about the tiniest thing done or said by him, when he comes home from work hungry and tired, there is no dinner waiting for him. Her regular practice of inflicting punishment upon him is to prepare the evening meal early, command us to eat our dinner, and then eradicate every indication that a meal had been prepared and eaten. The dishes are washed, the pots scrubbed, the stove cleaned and the floor swept. She commands us to keep our mouths shut about eating dinner.

Tearfully I swallow the food, as it threatens to lodge in my throat, while whispering among ourselves about how cruel she is. Daddy has gone to work all day, and now he's coming home to nothing to eat. I am trying to save some of my food for him, but she discovers my plan and gives the food to the dog, after giving me a swift lick. He comes home from work, washes his hands and sits down at the table, waiting for his dinner. No scents or sounds come from the kitchen.

"What's going on?" he asked. "No dinner tonight?"

That's the opening she has been waiting for; she lunges at him screaming about his inability to provide for the family. There is no money to buy food. How dare you ask for dinner?" I am crying at the injustice to my dad. As soon as it is safe to talk, I tell Daddy about what she made us do and how sorry I am to have eaten without leaving him something to eat. I tell him that I tried to save him some of my dinner, but she gave it to the dog. He looks at my tear-stained face, wipes the tears away and does his best to reassure me. "Don't worry; it's not your fault. You are not responsible for what your mother does." Slowly he gets up from the table, goes out the door and walks down the street to the corner shop. There he buys himself a bun and a wedge of cheese, or a loaf of bread and a can of sardines. Not only for him; but enough for all of us. I love my Daddy.

I graduate from Pembroke Hall Primary School, without sitting the Common Entrance Examination. On a Sunday morning a few months later, when the entire Island is abuzz and awake with the crackling of the pages of the newspaper, every teenage head apprehensively and excitedly bent over the pages, finding the high school of their choice. Looking with wide eyes for their names, they let out screams of joy or squeals of disappointments when their names are not printed among those accepted into the high schools for the upcoming school year. I remain in bed for as long as I can. I can hear the screams of the neighbors children. They are outside on the streets, shouting to each other the names of the high schools into which they have been accepted. Someone is knocking on the gate, calling my name.

"Marcia which school did you pass for? Where are you going to go to school?"

I hide inside the house, openly crying my heart out. I had not even been afforded the opportunity to fail the exam. My life is over. I feel like a failure, too ashamed to show my face again.

But I must show my face. It's the first day of school, and I am ashamed to be seen by the high-school students. I hate this aqua uniform, I think that everyone who sees me is thinking, "Oh, you poor thing. You are a failure. You did not pass the common entrance exam, and you are going to a secondary school, where you will get a second-class education."

I want to be wearing a grey tunic with a white shirt and red tie, or a tan shirt tucked into pleated, blue skirt, boasting a matching blue tie. I want to be wearing anything except this aqua garb. I keep my head down , trying to melt into the element as doors are opened and fresh faced students, eyes sparkling with the excitement of the first day of high school, rush out to meet their new world.

It's my first day of Secondary school. I mingle with the new students, each one seeming more interesting than the one before. I am wondering what each person's story of why they ended up here instead of at a high school will be. I take a deep breath, wipe the tears from my eyes, find my class and settle into a seat. This is where I will spend the next three years. I might as well stop feeling sorry for myself and make the best of the situation.

In my attempts to appear normal, I commit the unpardonable sin of talking to strangers. Not only have I spoken to new people, but I have made a new friend at school. On our walk home, we exchange school supplies. I sling her red school bag over my shoulder, while she hugs my new folder to her chest. We fully intend to return each other's stuff at the corner where we will part company. I will arrive home carrying something that does not belong to me. It's only after our parting that I discover the mistake. I have no clue about her whereabouts, no idea where she lives.

Mother notices me before I reach the gate. Her piercing eyes notice that I'm carrying a school bag, not a folder. She had not bought me a bag. Only God can help me now.

"Good evening, Mama."

Narrowing her eyes she grills me, "Whose bag is that? Where did you get it from?"

Quaking in my shoes, the explanation forms in my mind but is never uttered.

"Get out of here and don't come back until you find the person to whom that belongs. I sent you to school to learn, not to make friends."

"But..." I stammer

"Gal, don't make me kill you tonight. Go find the girl and give her back her bag. Don't come back until you have what I sent you to school with."

She storms into the house and slams the door behind her.

I walk back to the home of three students who attended the same primary school that I did, asking the different girls if they know where the new girl at school, Beverly Brown, lived. No one knows. I wander the streets aimlessly, crying, I don't know what to do. It begins to get dark. I drift back home, bag still in tow. One of my sisters open the door letting me into the house.

"Did you find the owner of the bag?" Mother bellows.

"No Mama, I don't know where she lives, but I'll return it in the morning."

The left hand hidden behind her back flashes forward, holding the dreaded club (three lengths of black electrical wire twisted together and formed into the shape of a walking cane) rock steady. A torrent of blows rain down on my head, shoulders, arms and legs with such force that I stagger falling backward. As I fall she kicks me in the stomach, stomping on me.

The beating is vicious. After she has satisfied herself I lay in a bloody pile on the floor, whimpering like a wounded animal.

Daddy arrives home a few minutes after the blows stopped coming. I am still lying where she left me.

"What have you done to the child?" he demanded "What did she do to make you beat her like this?" He bends down to help me up.

"I sent her to school with a folder and she comes back home with a school bag. I didn't buy her a bag. I am tired of telling her to leave people and their things alone."

"Vira, is that any reason to beat the child like this? Isn't she going back to school tomorrow? It must have been a mistake…"

"Mistake nothing. What is she doing with what does not belong to her? I have spent my life teaching them not to want what other people have, and on the first day of school she shows up with a bag belonging to some girl. If you touch her tonight you will get your share."

Daddy continues helping me up. She loses control of herself and a barrage of blows and curse words come down on him. He ignores her, paying attention to me. I'm bleeding from my face, arms and legs, and can barely get on my feet from the pain in my stomach. He does his best to help me get cleaned up while comforting me. We both get our beatings that night. With no compassion in any of her bones, she makes me attend school the next day. What a sight I am. The teachers question me about my appearance, and the children laugh and snicker behind my back. I make excuses, hiding the tears as best as I can.

My mother offers me no love, but my father is warm, loving and kind. He is a little on the stocky side with a balding head, and the soft brown hair around the sides of his head is often being brushed by one of his children. His light brown eyes fascinate us when they twinkle with mischief, as the children gather around him nightly on a canvas cot under the starry sky. He recounts stories of his life as a child in the country. He delights in telling us scary stories of ghosts and spirits in the fields, of rolling calves, and all types of strange creatures of the dark. We laugh and are allowed to be children, often too scared to go to sleep after story time.

Daddy is a lover of mangos, especially the variety called 'Number Eleven.' It's natural sugar and soft textured skin is delicious, and an abundance of juice flows freely from the moment your teeth sink into its skin, piercing the flesh hidden within. The only problem with these mangoes is that, because of their sweetness, they produced worms on the inside when fully ripe. Daddy finds a way to disregard these little invertebrates. He gets himself two or three mangos and waits until it's dark. Then he gets himself a plastic bag for the discarded seed, then he gets a chair and sits outside in the dark and enjoy his mangos. We ask about his behavior and he explains.

"This is the only way to eat and enjoy mangos. In the dark; where everything tastes good and you can't see anything."

"Daddy, you are so crazy!" His children tease him.

Regardless of what's going on between my parents. Daddy can always be counted on to remember us. At the end of each day he returns home from work with something in his hand or in his pocket for the children. He brings home mangos, apples, pears, plums, and cherries – anything that's in season. If he doesn't have a bag in his hand, we know there's something in his pockets. He comes through the gate and all of us run to greet him. He stands there with his arms above his head as we ravish through his pockets, searching to find the treasures he brings us. A candy is sufficient. It's not the size or value of what he brings home, it's the fact that he loves us enough to think about us, to make us feel wanted. I am grateful to him. It says to me that regardless of how badly my mother treats me, at least one parent loves me.

Christmas is a very special time for us. Daddy doesn't have money to buy us expensive toys but he does his best to make us happy. Mother knows how to sew, and she makes most of our clothes. Without exception each one of us has a new dress for Christmas morning. It becomes a tradition for the family; as the sun rises, and everything comes to life, we are awakened to strains of music. Daddy loves music and plays his harmonica or the keyboard incessantly. After an early breakfast, all of us get dressed and off we go to Christmas Market.

It's held on the streets of Kingston, where hundreds of sellers display their festive wears for the passers-by, and the smell of fruitcakes, baked ham, sorrel, potato and plum puddings wafts through the air and tickles our nostrils. We revel in the sights and sounds. But our real purpose for being here is for each child to choose a toy. Dolls, fire engines, trucks, doll houses, inflatable plastic Santa's, reindeers, elves... all manner of objects are on display. We return home weath each of us clutching our object of choice.

I love my Daddy. He is the stabilizing force in my life, but he's no match for his wife. He does his best to provide for the family and protect his children, but he can't escape her wrath.

Chapter Three

SOLD FOR A FISTFUL OF DOLLARS

M y mother's influential friend (who is also my godfather) owns a beautiful home on the hill in one of St. Andrew's elite neighborhoods. His position in the country's government is extolled, along with how good he has been to our family. I'm introduced to him and told that he is my godfather, and should be called Uncle Nowington. The family begins making regular visits to his other plush home in another well-heeled neighborhood. The servants cater to me, especially after I'm introduced as "Miss Marcia, Uncle Nowington's goddaughter."

I love visiting the kitchen; there I can have whatever I wish from the refrigerator. We get to take rides in big cars driven by men who open the doors for us. I feel rich and important. I feel good when Uncle Nowington takes me on his lap, asking me about school, reminding me to do well so I can achieve success in the future. Then he gives me $20 bills from his wallet, telling me to buy myself something special from him.

Uncle Nowington is a very important man: one of the leaders of the Island, a Minister in the government. When he appears on television making long speeches or having a debate with other ministers, we sit with open mouths, watching in awe as he and the others make all types of rules and regulations for the Island. To be known and be related to him is great. I tell all of my peers who he is, feeling special when they treat me with more respect because I am related to the Honorable M.H. Nowington, Minister of Government.

Often, while visiting the home in Englewood, our mother takes us out into the front yard, telling us to look up to the hill ahead of us. Magnificent homes rise up out of the blasted rocks, and there nestled among the foliage is the one we are trying to get a glimpse of.

"Do you see it? The yellow one, that's the ministerial home of your godfather." This sounds important, but it's lost on me.

One Sunday morning, a few months after my 12th birthday, my mother tells me to take a bath and get dressed because we are going out. She lays out my best Sabbath dress for me to wear. This must be important. Church clothes are never worn to anyplace, except church. For the first time in my life, Mother straightens my hair with the pressing comb. I feel like a grown up. All dressed up with long, smooth, pressed hair falling down my back.

"Where are you going?" my sisters ask.

"I don't know Mama just told me to get dressed."

They admire my new hairdo and wonder out loud when theirs will be straightened also.

Although it's Sunday, Daddy has gone to work to earn overtime pay. In silence, my Mother and I travel to a mysterious place. We board two buses; the last one takes us up on a hill. "Where are we going?" I wonder, but know better than to ask. I follow directions: do as I am told and go where I'm sent. My upbringing taught me to be seen but not heard. I ask no questions. Like a lamb, I'm silently led to the slaughter.

We exit the bus and walk a short distance up a private road past a few beautiful homes, then enter through the gate of one of them. Mama speaks to me for the first time since leaving home.

"This is your godfather's ministerial home, the one we tried showing you from his Avondale home. He has been good to the family and I want you to do whatever he tells you to. Do you hear me?"

"Yes, Mama." I can't possibly think of what I would be told to do. I am excited to be in such a grand place as a ministerial home.

The minister himself warmly greets us. He kisses my mother on the cheek and complements me on how nicely I have grown, and how pretty I am. He ushers us to the verandah where he serves us cool drinks and cake, explaining that all the help have gone home for the weekend. He and Mama chat while I tentatively explore the place.

I lightly touch the piano keys; run my hand over the soft chairs and look at the beautiful pictures on the walls. I soak up the newness of it all, trying to remember everything, so I can tell my sisters every detail. There is a peculiar smell, not unpleasant, just strange. I sniff the air trying to make a connection with something. I can't do it.

About an hour into the visit, I hear Mama calling me. I answer and come running from the living room which I had been exploring, onto the back verandah. She tells me to go with my godfather. He gets up from the chair and tells me to follow him, because he has something to show to me. I follow him through the large sitting room, and up three steps, which leads onto the second floor where the bedrooms are located. He opens the first door on the left telling me to go in. I obey. It's a large bedroom with its own bathroom. It's his bedroom. He offers me a seat on the edge of the bed and I sit down. He questions me about school.

"How are you doing in school? Are you getting good grades? What's your favorite subject? Are you being a good girl?"

I answer all his questions. He then begins running his hand over my newly pressed hair, telling me how pretty I am and how nice my hair look. I thank him. His hand travels to my knee and begins a journey to... where? I don't want to know. I shift my body, moving my legs away from him. He roughly pulls them back, telling me to be a good girl.

I know that this is wrong: he should not be touching my legs, attempting to get his hands under my skirt. I pull my skirt down further, adjusting my body further away from him. He yanks up my skirt and tries sticking his hand between my legs. Tears are running down my face. I jump up from the bed running for the door.

"No, please let me go back outside to Mama".

He grabs my arm shoving me back down on the bed. I'm crying loudly.

"What are you doing?" I ask. He ignores my question trying to get on top of me. "Stop it. Uncle Nowington, please stop it."

Cursing under his breath, he opens the door; I immediately jump off the bed thinking he is allowing me to go free. Instead, he sticks his head out the door and calls my mother. I'm standing directly behind him crying. Surely she will rescue me from this wretched man.

Mother treads the stairs to the room. He steps halfway out the door to speak to her.

"Talk to her. She is not cooperating."

My mother walks into the room. I look up at her expectantly. She slaps my face, yelling.

"What is the matter with you? Didn't I tell you to do as you are told? Get back in that room and don't make me have to come back up here or you will be sorry."

Turning on her heels, she waltzes out of the room. He comes back in, and this time he locks the door behind him pocketing the key.

"Get on the bed." He orders.

I stand my ground, crying. He grabs my arm, viciously pulling me toward the bed, pushing me down on it. With all my strength I fight, but could not fight off the advances of a 62-year-old man, who has my mother's permission to rape me. He's trying to yank off my panties and I'm fighting to keep my legs tightly crossed. I sob loudly from deep within. He pushes my legs apart, letting go of my right leg. I immediately draw it up to my chest. He grabs my heel pulling it back down. He uses his right knee to keep my legs down and apart. He now has me pinned down on the bed, my panties have been thrown someplace and my legs are apart. I'm crying. He uses his right hand to guide himself as he plunges his manhood into my 12-year-old virgin body. I scream as the air rushed out of my lungs. He firmly clasps his hand over my mouth. I bite his hand, but that has no effect on him. He is bent on raping me and I'm powerless to stop him.

Only the fire of hell could be this painful. Every part of my body feels as if it's being consumed from within. I begin choking, while thrashing my legs around to get him off and out of my body. I beat against his chest twisting my head from side to side, trying to free his hand. But all my efforts are in vain. Effortlessly he holds me in a tight grip. My heart is so full of fear and hate that I think I'm about to explode. "Somebody help me. O God, help me. Why is this happening to me? Why did my mother bring me here for this to happen? God where are you? Please rescue me out of this."

"You are a feisty little one, aren't you," he mutters, as he violently and viciously continues to rape me.

When he's through ravishing my body, he slowly removes his hand from my mouth, telling me to be quiet. By then, I'm in too much pain to be anything but quiet. He swings off the bed going, to his bathroom where he cleans himself. A few minutes later he emerges with a wet washcloth. The sheets had been pulled up to my neck trying to hide myself from him. He yanks the sheet from my hands, pushes my legs apart and uses the washcloth to clean the blood and his fluid off of me. Turning my head away from him, I allow the tears to run down my cheeks soaking the pillow and settling in a pool under my head. "Stay where you are for a little while; then get dressed and come join us." He picks up his pants and underwear off the floor, laying them on a chair, and sits down on the bed next to my head.

I turn my head to the other side as I lay there in agony. My body is throbbing and I'm unable to move. My insides feel as if they have been churned in a blender.

He's stroking my leg. I pull them away from his hand. "You need to learn to be obedient, and then you won't get hurt. Your mother and I have big plans for you. You will be groomed to be a part of all this one day, but you must be obedient. Keep your mouth shut about this and anything else that happens within these walls. Do you understand me?"

Unable to speak, I nod in the affirmative. He lights and smokes a cigarette, then he takes a drink from a glass. Setting the glass down, he gets on the bed and lies down beside me. I turn away onto my side, quietly sobbing.

"This is the type of behavior I am talking about." he said, as he roughly grabs my shoulders, forcing me onto my back. To my horror he get himself over me, and begins raping me again. I am in the belly of hell with the worst creature on earth. I'm transfixed on the pain. This cannot be happening. Surely it must be a very bad nightmare from which I will wake up. But it is not a dream and I am wide awake.

Like a lioness I fight, tearing at his hair, biting his shoulders, beating on his back. He doesn't even flinch from the blows. Again, I lose the fight. I beg God to take my life, because the pain is too much for me to endure. How can this be happening to me? From somewhere deep within the recesses of my soul, survival instinct kicks in. My mind removes itself from what's happening to me. My body is being raped but my mind takes flight elsewhere, to a safer place. I'm singing, "Jesus loves the little children all the children of the world, red and yellow black and white they are precious in his sight, Jesus loves the little children of the world."

Why doesn't my mother help me? Does she know what's going on in the bedroom? Of course she knows. My 'loving' mother had dressed me up, pressed my hair, and taken me on a mysterious trip to a big, beautiful ministerial home. She presented me to a powerful minister within the government of the country, my godfather. She seated herself in a comfortable chair, sipping a cool drink, eating delicious cake, and enjoying the ambiance of her surroundings while I am being raped a few feet away.

As I ponder this, I realize that this was not an accident; it had been planned between my mother and my godfather. I have become a victim of my mother's evil scheming. My mind cannot process the enormity of the situation at this time. The only thing I know is that an evil worse than death has touched me in the worst way. Something worst than death has crawled into my soul, taking up residence within my very existence, and my mother is in agreement with it.

He satisfies himself, then he cleans himself off again. As he is getting dressed, he instructs me to get dressed and join them on the veranda. He walks out of the room as if nothing had happened. Through the open window I hear him join my mother on the verandah. They engage in conversation and laughter. Gingerly I get off the bed, testing the level of pain that shoots through me. I hunch over for a couple minutes, and then drag myself into the bathroom. Looking down at myself, the sight of blood and my red swollen vulva, shocks me. The pain is excruciating. I clean myself, wincing at every touch. Pulling my underwear up, the touch of the nylon against my skin is unbelievably painful. I leave them hanging down as far as I can.

Bawling in gut-wrenching agony, I continue getting dressed, staggering to lean against the bathroom door. I don't know what to do. How am I going to face my mother? I feel dirty and ashamed. What am I going to do? Trying to regain my composure, I wash my face, comb my hair, straighten my dress and waddle out of the room. I go into the kitchen and pour myself a glass of water. Then as carefully as I can, I sit down on the edge of a chair in the living room. I'm expecting my mother to come see how I was, but she never came. She does not cast one single glance in my direction.

Almost an hour later, my mother decides it's time to go. She calls my name. I answer, but don't move. They prepare to separate, entering the room. I stand up. Standing there with my head hung down low and my legs apart, I wish the ground could open up and swallow me. Right there before my eyes, my godfather takes his wallet from his back pocket, removes a few $100 bills, and pays my mother for the service I had rendered. At that moment, the realization hits me:

I had been sold. Sold by my mother for a fistful of dollars.

Chapter Four

BETRAYALS

As Mama and I leave the ministerial home, thoughts swirl around in my mind like a cyclone. What should I do? Should I tell her about what had happened? Should I ask her why she had taken me up there? Should I tell her how much he had hurt me? Did she have previous knowledge of his intentions? Was she a part of his plan? Walking is difficult. The throbbing and pain from between my legs, up into my stomach, is still very intense, causing me to lag behind, unable to keep up with her long strides. After walking for a few minutes to the bus stop, I work up the nerve to say something.

"Mama," I mutter. That is the only word which escapes my lips. "Shut up," She answers, glaring at me. "I don't want to hear anything from you."

I close my mouth and keep it closed. I know that the events will never be spoken about. The shame and pain is swelling up in me, becoming more and more intense as we walk silently along. I begin feeling like a pressure cooker. I hope I don't explode.

My sisters are waiting for us to return home. When we walk in the door, they wait for mother to leave the room and begin asking. "Where did you go? What happened? Why do you look so sad, didn't you have fun?" Forcing a smile, I promise to give details later, and head for the bathroom. Gently, I press a cold wet washcloth to the swollen area. I do everything conceivable to stop the pain. Nothing works. Again, I dry my tears, straighten my clothing, and go to bed, staying there for the remainder of the evening.

Betrayals

This was only the first of many trips I make, accompanied by my mother to the man on the hill. It becomes almost a ritual. She presses my hair, orders me to get dressed, and we travel to the home. I sit in the living room quietly crying. When he is ready, he grabs my arm and takes me to his bedroom. There I'm raped. He doesn't call my mother to slap my face anymore. He does the beatings. He pulls me up on my knees, pushing my face down into the pillows. When he enters me from behind, I scream bloody murder. He punches me in my back, slapping my buttocks. He turns me onto my back and slaps my face several times. My mouth begins bleeding. He tells me to shut up if I don't want to get hurt. I learn to remain still. Fighting is useless: I never win. My mind finds refuge someplace else, disconnecting myself from the pain in my body. Mama waits for him to return from raping me, then I hear them laughing and talking. After a while, he pays her, and we make the silent trip home.

Two years later, when Bridget, my younger sister turns 12, the pattern is repeated. I know what's going on. When they return home, I look at her with pity, but I'm unable to help her. I wonder if she, too, had been raped by my godfather on the hill. But I don't dare venture to ask her where they went and what happened? I am too ashamed, and too afraid of being killed by Mama.

I don't know when Mother sacrificed Cheryl. She tells me that she remembers being barely 12 years old when she is taken up to Uncle Nowington's house. Mother takes her to the bedroom, leaving her there at his mercy. He begins touching her. She begins to cry. She remembers being so ashamed, and conscious of her torn underwear, that she stands there immobilized, offering no resistance to his probing hands. Cheryl is raped with her mother lounging just a few feet away.

She is out of daughters to be sold. I wonder what will she do now?

I am under duress: all I have ever wanted is the love of my mother. More than life itself, I desire the open arms of my mother. I would give my right arm if she asks for it as payment for her love. I will do anything to make her love me. I feel like an alien in a world where mothers love their children, and children adore and revere their mothers. I have spent years trying to figure out what I had done wrong, causing me to be devoid of so precious an affection. As a child, I felt so inadequate. If I was not good enough for my mother to love, then who could possibly love me? To compensate for the absence of her love I pour out my emotions to my father and my sisters and brother. As desperately as I need my mother's love, I seek the love I desire in my younger siblings.

My sisters and I talk among ourselves, promising never to treat our children the way she has treated us. I decide to do the exact opposite of everything she has done. I have no desire to be like her. I am afraid of inheriting any trace of her disposition, and quickly squash anything noticeable in my behavior which displays the slightest reminder of her. If someone tells me that I look like my mother, it is quickly denied. "No, I don't. I look like my father." I laugh at a joke, and someone commented that I sound like my mother. Instantly I set to work, changing the pitch and range of my voice. I want to be nothing like her, bearing no resemblance to the woman who brought me into the world.

I finally realize that my survival depends upon finding a way to cope with my inner emotional turmoil. I begin burying myself in fantasy books. I keep them hidden in my textbooks, pretending to study, while instead devouring great flights of fantasy and fairy tales. I lock myself in the bathroom, ignoring the knocks for as long as I can. It's often the only quiet place I can find to read in peace. I begin writing on everything I can find. I write on scraps of paper, on napkins, on my arm. I find writing to be the much-needed release of the tension that builds up inside of me – like opening a pressure valve, keeping me from exploding.

Janice finds solace in writing poetry. Her book of poetry, *Bareface Pickney*, has earned her the recognition she deserves. The following is an example of one of her poems relating her attempts to find answers to the same questions I have been asking:

A CHILD'S WISH
By Alicia Janice McLaren

A very hard thing for me to do
is to write a poem in praise of you
for though I try, we all know
that love and tenderness you do not show

I would love to tell my friends
how your children you always defend
how you rocked us on your knees
in love with you we'd always be

I dream of telling everyone
That you will always understand
That individual we'll forever be
That you accepted "radical me"

That you loved us no matter what
You thanked God for whatever you got
You nurtured us with love and care
We always knew that you were near

I hope and pray that I could say
You showed us tenderness everyday
You guided us with the facts of life
You never threatened with a knife

You gave us positive views of you
The wonderful things you always do
You hugged and kissed us in formative days
You talked us out of childhood fears

But sad to say I cannot lie
My childhood days will make me cry
I cannot write the traditional lines

The Odyssey Of Survival

Caregivers come in many kinds

So though I desperately want to say
I love you more with each passing day
I have to hold my pen awhile
For there is bitterness though a child

So please try now to make amends
We do so want to be your friend
Your children want to take care of you
To turn the clock and start anew
For our days on earth could be few.

Chapter Five

GOOD AND EVIL, TRUTH AND LIES

The highly renowned Rev J.C. Palmer, Evangelist for the Seventh-day Adventist Conference, will be arriving in Kingston to conduct a four-week crusade under the big tent at Marverly Park. Excitement fills the air as the news is voiced throughout the church community. The impending arrival of the preacher caused a stir in the hearts of the religious, and awe in the eyes of the teenagers.

The flyers proclaim, "Get ready to be blessed, for the mighty man of God is coming to town and lives will be changed. Prepare to attend nightly meetings under the big tent."

I have never attended an evangelistic crusade, especially one held under a tent. Excited, I await the commencement of these meetings. Rev. Palmer does not disappoint his audience. He has the crowd the first night. He skillfully teaches the people about God's love for them, about His forgiveness, and plan of salvation for each one of us. He tells us how Christ came to earth to save us from our sins, and our past sins will be forgiven if we repent. To complement his teachings, he brought in some of the best musicians and singers to minister to us. I am transfixed by the encouraging words of salvation and accompanying music.

My family attends the meetings as often as possible. Patricia and I are allowed to attend the meetings by ourselves on weeknights. Our parents are too tired and the others are considered too young. After meetings conclude each evening, a couple of the young men walk us home, being careful to retreat just before turning that last corner where they would be observed by our mother, who is religiously sitting upon her bed. She is hidden behind the curtains, watching through the window to see if we dare have anyone walk into her line of vision. Carefully, we protect our companions, enjoying the unexpected freedom of being out of the house at least two nights weekly.

The teachings caused a stirring in my heart, and a deep longing to experience the everlasting and unconditional love of God. My life has been so debased and void of love that the prospect of a God loving me enough to have died for me seems surreal. I crave to be loved in that fashion. Although I have been attending church for years, this is the first time I have been exposed to the true nature of God. The Reverend's words have a great impact on my sister and me. We want to hear more about this God who loves us so much that He had given up his life, dying on a cross to save us into His kingdom so we could live with him for eternity. We certainly needed someone to love us, and God sounded like He was the only one who could do so. Patricia and I, along with many others decide to give our lives to God. When the appeal is made for those who wanted to be baptized we are among the first ones who respond to the call.

The response to the appeal is so great that the leaders decide that the baptism would have to be held at a beach, for the facilities at the tent could not accommodate the volume of new believers. A trip to the beach was always a treat, regardless of the occasion. One week later on a beautiful Sunday morning, three chartered buses filled with sinners seeking freedom and forgiveness of our sins are loaded up and head for the Gunboat Beach. We sing the songs of redemption and praise as the buses roll along filled with people, happy in our newfound Lord.

The mass baptism of about 300 is a great success. No one drowns, and we are rejoicing and singing even louder on the return trip. The crusade ends with hundreds of new converts being added to the church. The existing congregations in the surrounding areas gladly accept some of the new members, but there is still an overflow with no church of our own to attend. The conference of the denomination hears about this problem and sends a representative to assess the needs of the people. They give permission for a new church to be built. The property is acquired and plans for the construction of a suitable house of worship begins.

Daddy, the carpenter, volunteers to build the church along with most of the other men. Sundays and every evening after work, this dedicated band of men hammers, pounds, saws and nails. In no time at all, the beginnings of a structure appear out of the ground. Up it goes, taking shape, until on a memorable Sabbath morning, our newly formed congregation has the immense pleasure of worshipping in our very own church. My family is proud to be among the founding members of this brand new church.

It is still not much of a church at this stage. The men have erected four walls and cut openings for windows, but no windows have been installed yet. When the wind blows up the dust, we get dusty; when it rains, everyone gathers in the middle of the sanctuary to avoid getting wet. The seats are long slabs of plank nailed down on stumps, with no supporting backs. The floor is dirt and the roof is zinc, which leaks at the joints. But we love our little church. It has been built with the sweat of our congregation. It belongs to us. The congregation grows until we are appointed a leader. Pastor Woodburn, a kind grandfatherly man, becomes our shepherd. He leads his little band of sheep very well, and we love him.

Across the street from our church is another church, which belongs to a strange religious sect. While we worship quietly and piously with serene bowed heads, this church is loud and noisy. On Sunday nights, both churches hold services, but we have a difficult time hearing our speakers as their shouts of praise drown out everything else. This type of worship fascinates the youth in the congregation. Ignoring the orders of our leaders and parents not to enter the premises, we creep silently across the street to watch firsthand the happenings in this church. We watch with wide-eyed amazement as they jump and prance around, the women having to be wrapped in sheets to prevent total exposure of themselves to all onlookers, and the men falling on the ground shouting, while the children seem delirious with whatever possesses them.

We can't get enough of these performances, and attend Sunday night services mainly to watch these people. The trouble we get into when the adults of our congregation discover us peering through the door and windows at "the crazy people" doesn't stop us; we are fascinated by this type of worship. Who are they worshipping? Is it

51

the same God who we ever so quietly and piously worship? And to whom is he listening. Can he hear them better because they shout so loudly, and is he able to hear us over the din of their noise?

Our new congregation needs everyone to participate in the services of the church. I jump into action, becoming involved in many areas. I teach children's Sabbath School, and become the secretary of youth services called Adventist Youth, (AY). My parents, who both sing well, become choir members. (Mother sings soprano and Daddy has a deep bass voice). I don't know what happened to my voice – I am tone deaf.

Another good thing comes out of the new congregation. I find a friend. I am 14 years old, and somehow we are drawn to each other. I admire this tall, young girl who is three years my senior. Kathy and I became close. Her parents joined the church in its early days. She has a younger sister who is Bridget's age, and they also form a friendship as well. This is good. We become a foursome. We whisper to each other on Sabbaths, and soon realize that we are both being abused by our mothers. Kathy lives with her mother and stepfather, and is disliked by her mother. Although we compared notes on their treatment of us, I am very careful never to mention the sexual abuse which my mother has sanctioned. The shame of it makes me feel almost responsible and I am very afraid of anyone discovering what has been happening to me.

Kathy is allowed to visit our home on Sabbath afternoons – it's the only day that strangers are allowed into the home. On Fridays, Mama spends all day preparing the meal for Sabbath lunch. She cooks rice and peas, chicken and vegetables, and the sweet potato pudding sends the mouth-watering aroma throughout the house as it's baked the old fashion way of hell on top hell on the bottom and hallelujah in the middle. This is all washed down with homemade carrot, sour sop, or cucumber juice. I can't wait to return from church to dive into the sumptuous meal.

Sometimes I have the rare treat of visiting Kathy's home which is huge and has fruit trees in the backyard, including different varieties of mangos which grow in abundance. I always leave her home with a bag of mangos, to everyone's delight.

I'm being beaten in Kathy's presence. The simple infraction of contradicting my mother on a point resulted in being kicked to the ground and pounded upon until my blood is spilled. It's Sabbath afternoon; Mama had pealed her lungs out on the choir earlier, shouting Amen to the sermon on love and forgiveness.

Now she slaps and spits in my face. A punch to the stomach folds me over in pain. As I bend over from the impact, she punches me in the back. I remember hearing Kathy begging her to stop.

"Sis Mac, are you going to kill her?" she asks.

Ranting and screaming that I think I'm a big woman, she kicks me, and as I fall to the ground she stomps on my sides. Kathy tries pulling her off of me, but she is roughly pushed away. When my mother has satisfied herself, she administers one last kick, then walks away, leaving me a bloody mess, with a threat to kill me later. My friend kneels at my side trying to comfort me. She helps me up to my feet and to the bathroom to clean my face. My tears mingle with blood and stream down my face. I lean on my friend's shoulder, whimpering like a trampled puppy. She comforts me, dries my tears, and stems the blood flow. I compose myself and we try to hide the bruises as best we can before leaving home to attend AY at church. Slowly we walk along the road, trying desperately to hide my distressed, pathetic state from passers-by.

The knowledge that Sabbath is coming makes it a little easier for me to endure the hardships of the week. Church spells a little freedom for me. There I am reminded that no matter how bad things are, I shouldn't give up because God loves and cares about me At times I find it difficult to believe that God really cares about me. The question of why He allows such awful things to happen to me is always on my lips. I constantly question God in prayer. But there is no response. I am begging Him to help me, to get me out of my situation, but there is no answer, and my situation doesn't change. Still, I find some comfort in the words of the pastor, and it's these words of encouragement which keep me going more than anything else. I keep praying and hoping that God will do something to make my life better. I don't know what to expect, but I'm convinced He will hear and help me. I just hope it's soon. Before Mama kills me.

Time seems to drag on, as my life becomes worse from abuse and misuse. Enduring the evil of my godfather and the wretched hate of my mother, I begin to lose hope and faith in God. He had seemed so real and so close to me. During those meetings under the tent, I felt as if He held me in his arms. When I was baptized at the Gunboat beach, I felt as if I was in His very presence. When I worship at church with the other believers, my heart soars heavenward. What I can't understand is why has He turned his back on me? What have I done to make Him hide His face from me, allowing these two people to commit such evils against me?

Over time, as the rapes continue and the beatings keep coming, I become so disenchanted with life that I think God must have given up on me. So I give up on Him. I go to church because I'm forced to, but my heart has become hard and dead. I refuse to have anything to do with the God of my mother. I no longer feel like one of God's children. My life is on a slippery slope to hell, with nothing to stop my headlong descent. I keep attending church, and I even enjoy the activities, but my heart has become a solid rock.

The years following my baptism are terrible. I had hoped that by becoming a baptized member of God's church my mother would stop selling me to my godfather. But my hopes have been dashed. I had hoped that she would now reconsider, and change her actions as she observes my interest and participation in church activities, but she is bent on continuing what she had started.

The day of my first rape was the beginning of many years of rape and abuse by this man. With more frequency than I can or care to record, my mother orders me to get myself ready, and the now - familiar trip to the ministerial home on the hill is made. There is no use protesting – it will only result in my being abused twice, first by her beating, and later being raped by my godfather.

The chauffeured car frequently pulls up at the gate. The chauffeur gets out, a letter is handed to my mother, and I am ordered to take a bath, get dressed and present myself where I have been ordered to appear. At times I'll be there for two days at a time, missing school if he desires my presence during the week. Upon my return, Daddy would question me as to my whereabouts. I'm told to simply tell him that I was at Uncle Nowington's. I think Daddy is suspicious of what is going on, but he accepts my answers. He touches me on my shoulder, telling me that it's not good to miss so many days from school.

My eyes fill up with tears, I long to confide in him; to tell him what's really going on, but I fear for my life too much. I live in constant fear: afraid of my mother killing me, afraid to tell my father what has been going on at Uncle Nowington, afraid to talk to my sisters, afraid to confide in my friend. Fear has a firm grip on me.

During the election campaign one year, both Bridget and I are sent with him to the parish that he represented on the Island. After one week of taking nightly turns in his bed (of which we never speak to each other during the days) we make the return trip to Kingston. It's a rare occurrence when he drives himself. During the journey, my sister and I are sitting in the back seat, entertaining ourselves. Looking at us through the rear view mirror, he orders one of us to climb over the seat and get in the passenger seat next to him.

Bridget and I look at each other, but neither one move. He barks his order a second time, but we remain seated. He pulls the car over onto the shoulders of the road and get out. He yanks the door open dragging me out of the back seat, shoving me into the front seat. He climbs back in cursing me for my disobedience and insolence, while he tries to get his fingers inside of me to pleasure himself. Sitting stiffly in the seat and keeping my legs tightly closed, I fight him, refusing to allow him entry. He removes his hand in disgust and orders me to get back in the rear of the car. He summons Bridget to take my place in the front. At the end of the journey we are unceremoniously dropped off at home.

I am 15 years old, about to graduate from secondary school, and my mother takes me to him. He has his way with me, and she receives a handsome reward. I have five subjects to study at school, and want to go to college. I know it's going to be tough, but I want to try. My lifetime dream is to attend college, then law school to become a lawyer. Before graduation, when students are being prepared to take O- and A-level exams in hope of securing enough subjects to be considered likely applicants for acceptance into college, I'm told not to even bother thinking about that. Instead I am going to be sent to business school to learn business management skills, so I can be an assistant to my godfather in his political career. My ambitions are high, but they have been dashed. I have no way to pay for the classes or to support myself in college, so my dream becomes just that – a dream... another *bad* dream. My mother enrolls me in the Jamaica Commercial Institute, where I will learn to write and translate Pitman Shorthand, learn to type, file, keep records and other skills.

My entire life has been a bad dream – mostly a nightmare – out of which I have been struggling to awaken. But the fog of evil looms so dark and hangs so low over me that I can't seem to shake off the destructive hand that I have been dealt. I have not been able to achieve the level of success for which I have worked so hard and so long. My mother constantly berates me, always telling me that I will never achieve anything in life. I will never amount to much in life. I will never be successful.

On many, many occasions, when she gets particularly mad at her bunch of unwanted children, she removes her breasts from within her clothing, beat on them with her fist, place a burning match too close for comfort to her nipples, call upon God's name, then inform us that we are cursed forever, because we have caused our mother to "burn her breast for us." Am I cursed forever? Has God cursed me for the rest of my life?

Church... ahh church! During all those years of my mother selling me, compounded by her desire and attempts to kill me, she has never missed one Sabbath from church. She remains a fervent church attendee, and regardless of the beating endured a few hours earlier, I am required to wash my face, dry my eyes, get dressed, go to church., smile and be polite to all who speak to me.

The privilege of giving my most precious irreplaceable gifts given to me by God, reserved for my husband, has been taken away against my will. I will never be an innocent virgin on my wedding night. She has taken it away from me. My dream of walking out of my mother's house in the most beautiful white wedding dress, to meet my husband at the altar, with the blessing of my mother will never be realized. I must accept this, and hope that a young man will somehow still want to marry me, despite my being used.

I do not know what it feels like to be hugged by my mother and told, "I love you." I have never had the opportunity of sitting on Mama's knees, telling her about a problem, asking for her advice, and listening to her wisdom. I have not had the privilege of experiencing a mother's limitless love – that love which causes mothers to rise to the defense of their children, that love which makes a mother furious at the very indication that someone would entertain the thought of harming one of her children That love which, even if the child did wrong, will make you go to battle to protect your own flesh and blood. That love which makes a mother say, "You'll be better off if you hurt me instead of my child, because if you hurt my child I will kill you."

The opposite is true in my life: my mother creates situations which endanger my life, making me an easy target for the actions of unscrupulous men. She spends her life trying to kill me herself, creating an unstable, abusive, dysfunctional environment. I have not learnt how to love, how to trust, how to accept love from others. Like the chickens, I have spent my life scratching around on the ground, looking for a place to lay down my head and find rest. That rest has eluded me. I remain a sad, unloved, unwanted child, still grappling and finding no answer to the question.

Why does my mother hate me?

Both of my parents are very active in church, Mama more so. She teaches a Sabbath school class, sings on the choir, and is a deaconess. The truth is that Sabbath is the only happy day in my life. It's the only day that I can escape her wrath for a few hours, but God help me if I commit an infraction during this holy day; my skin will be peeled after the sacred hours are over. Even with this always hanging over my head, I still enjoy Sabbath.

Upon entering our home, no one can ever imagine how badly treated I am. Having people around brings out the best in me, so that my behavior is impeccable. I smile, serve the guests, enjoy the meal, and pretend that I live a normal life.

Thank God, regardless of how a child is treated, that child will grow into a teenager and ultimately into adulthood. By His grace I am growing up, and a small ray of hope flickers in my heart. I begin maturing, and slowly I begin to feel that if I have made it this far, I just might make it after all. I trudge through my days, trying to keep out of mother's way, struggling to maintain my sanity, keeping quiet about my situation at home. Maybe, just maybe, I might survive

Mama.

Patricia migrates to Canada, joining the older siblings there.

With Patricia's leaving, I become the oldest child in the home. The responsibilities grow. The preparation of meals for the family becomes mine. So does cleaning the house and ironing the clothes. Even Daddy's underwear has to be ironed, in addition to taking care of the younger children. We are still not allowed to associate with the neighborhood children, so we entertain ourselves in any way we can.

A new family moves into the house two doors down from us. The parents fight constantly, until one day the mother packs her bags and leaves the home, leaving behind five of the most pitiful little children I have ever seen. I am sorry for them. Their father is a drunk who leaves them alone all day long with no food in the house.

They stand at the fence looking at us. With wide, sad eyes they watch the other children playing on the street. Their hair is greasy and uncombed, and their clothes are filthy. In our mother's absence we share our food with them, handing it over the fence or through the gate. We are careful never to enter their premises, lest our mother hears about our trespassing from a nosey neighbor. We play ball games with them over the fence and try entertaining them as much as we can. I possess a good sense of time and am usually able to predict Mama's return from the market, or wherever she has gone.

One fateful day, the little girls look particularly filthy. I can smell their unwashed bodies across two fences. I decide that as soon as mother is safely out of the house I'll call the girls over, and clean them up as quickly as I can. Mama is safely through the gate and down the street, I give her a few minutes to talk to Miss Lewis, and get to the bus stop. One by one I call the little girls over, I shampoo their hair and, sitting of the front steps begin the tedious task of untangling the knots. I am down to the last one, becoming engrossed in my task, and to my detriment I lose track of time. Hearing a sound, I look up and there is Mama coming through the gate.

Darts of fire shoot from her eyes at me, and shivers of fear run down my spine. O God. I am dead now.

"What are you doing? What are these filthy children doing over here? Get out of my yard!" she screams. "And all of you get inside."

Everyone scatters. We march inside to face the wrath of mother.

This is a beating I will never forget.

"What do you think you are doing with those filthy children?"

"I was just trying to help them because they stink and their hair is so dirty and smelly."

"Who put you in charge of them? Are you their mother now?"

"No Mama."

"When I say you children are to stay inside, I mean you are to stay inside, do you understand?"

"Yes Mama."

Bam! She punches me, then she slaps and kicks me. I pick up my head, and she spits in my face. Why? All I had done was try to help a few needy children. This makes no sense to me. I love and care about children, and cannot understand why I'm being punished for lending a helping hand. But then I do not understand much of what my mother does.

Where is God? This is a fervent question on my lips and in my heart. Why doesn't he stop her cruelties? Why does he allow her to continue treating me so badly, while she piously attends church weekly, singing on the choir, teaching Sabbath school and presenting herself as a good person to the world? On several occasions, I ask my father why he chose her to be my mother, why couldn't he have chosen a nice person, someone like himself? He tries explaining to me how we would not be the same people if even one of our parents were different. I don't care. I just want a nice mother.

I am so tired of her cruelties that I begin hating her. I find myself wishing her dead, I am spending time thinking about ways to get rid of her. Somehow, in all of this, I am still very aware of the respect that should be shown to her as my mother. No matter what Mama does, regardless of how I complain about her behind her back, Bridget is always the voice of reason saying to me, "Stop it. She is still your mother." I do not understand. I know that God still expects me to respect her, but I don't have to love her, do I?

I am cooking the family's Sunday dinner. The red kidney beans are boiling in coconut milk on the stove and the chicken has been seasoned and is marinating on the kitchen counter. Mama is walking through the kitchen to the back yard with a load of dirty laundry in her arms. As she passes the stove, a piece of clothing catches on the handle of the pot in which the peas are boiling.

The pot comes crashing down off the stove, the boiling contents are spilling all over the kitchen floor, Mama loses her balance and goes down into the hot mixture. She screams as she lands on her back and the scalding liquid soaks through her clothing. We run to the kitchen, she is slipping in the milk, unable to get a grip. We get her to her feet, and there on the length of the back of her leg are kidney beans, embedded into her flesh.

I am bending over her, trying with all my might to get her up off the floor and out of the hot milk. Screaming that I am trying to kill her, she pushes me away from her. Bridget comes to the rescue, and together we get her up from the floor, onto a chair. Bridget picks the beans from her flesh, as she screams in pain. Her leg is swelling up quickly. I run for and return with a cold washrag, she yells in my face for me to get away from her.

I don't know what to do. My mother has been badly burnt, and she is blaming me for the accident. Then I remember my church youth leader, who lives a few streets over. I run all the way to his home, breathlessly explaining what has happened. He drops what he has been doing, walking quickly back home with me.

He applies soothing cold compress and ointment to the water blisters which have formed. Mama swears that I deliberately pulled the pot off the stove just as she passed by in order to kill her. I was not even in the kitchen, I defend myself. But she blames me for what happened, and promises to exact revenge on me as soon as she is able to move around again.

At church, I enjoy participating in a vibrant youth club, called "Pathfinders." I revel in the activities, the hiking, and campouts and singing around the campfire. I enjoy gazing up into the clear night sky and learning to identify some of the constellations. "That is Big Dipper, over there is Little Dipper. Look over there, do you see it? That's Orion." These lessons provide the distraction to my life that I need to survive. I love every moment of the grueling drill as the leader shouts, "Pathfinders, Ah-ten-tion!" Every right foot stomps down, and our arms are held stiffly at our sides. Pathfinders, forward march! Trying our best not to bump into each other, we move forward, hopefully arms are swinging in unison with the legs.

Early one Sunday morning, the club members and its leaders board a bus, and we are off to the Dunn's River beach for a day of fun and frolic in the warm waters, as they cascade down from the falls. Dreams of climbing the rocks to the top of the falls are on our lips. We are excited.

At the beach we receive last instructions, and off we go splashing into the water. One of the leaders takes a group of boys out for a diving lesson. Over and over they dive, breaking the surface again and again, perfecting the technique. They disappear from sight once again, counting the seconds to see how long they remain under. The students are up, we are expecting our leader to emerge any moment now. Wow he has been down there for a long time.

We are getting nervous, something is definitely wrong, he could not possibly hold his breath for so long. Someone begins screaming to the other leaders, they come running, jumping into the water, searching for a friend. Life guards join in the search, we are huddled together crying. Where is he, what has happened to him?

The search continues for what seems like an eternity. Then they make the grim pronouncement.

One of our leaders, a strong swimmer, is dead. He drowned during a routine diving lesson. Before our very eyes, he went down, and he never came back up. His pregnant wife is awaiting his return. What are we going to tell her?

How we cry as we pile back into the bus for the drive home, as the trip comes to an abrupt, sorrowful end. We cannot understand what happened. No one can explain it to us. One of our leaders is dead, and we are devastated.

His wife is inconsolable, and somehow the club manages to go on. Our leader died doing what he enjoyed, he will never be forgotten.

There is a very bad pain in my head. It began in my temples and exploded in my forehead. Its blinding effects is making it hard for me to open my eyes and focus, the light is making it worst, and when I force my eyes open there are black spots in front of them. I am trying to catch them, but can't focus. My God, I am going crazy. My head is killing me, I am nauseous and miserable.

Mama tells me to take two Phensic and go lie down. Hours later,

I am still in pain. She gives me a second dose, the next day I can't go to school because I can't get out of bed, I'm unstable on my feet and can't eat. Concerned, she gets me to the hospital. There I am examined with painful light into my eyes and many questions which I am doing my best to answer. I'm diagnosed with severe migraine headaches and hospitalized. After several shots, my head is still exploding, and now, even though I have been deprived of sleep, it's impossible for me to fall asleep. It's as if the ability to shut my brain down has left me. Day and night I lie there suffering in silence.

After a few days in the hospital, I'm sent home with a prescription for pain medication. Slowly the pain goes away, but my sleep does not return. If I am lucky, I'll get four hours of fitful rest. Will I ever be able to have a good night's sleep again?

I graduate from business school with Diploma in Secretarial and Business Studies. I am proficient in Pitman Shorthand and type 60 words per minute. Coupled with my English and other subjects, I am deemed acceptable to be in the employment of the minister. I become a working woman – the personal assistant to the Minister, my godfather and rapist.

The same chauffeured car, which, for the past four years frequently picks me up to be molested, now picks me up Monday through Friday for work. I work in his office, receive a salary and am driven home at the end of each work day. He has not lost his perverse interest in me, but due to the professional environment, his advancements have curtailed. I begin to blossom, smiling more, and making friends. I am almost like a normal teenager.

Henry, the Pathfinder club's leader, takes an interest in my family, but more so in me. He visits the home frequently, and with five club members under the same roof, there is plenty to discuss. His special interest in me is flattering and results in a friendship between us, which blossoms into puppy love on my part. Contact with the opposite sex has been fiercely forbidden. Henry is allowed into our home only because of his position in church. For a few months we whisper into each other's ears on the telephone from the office, all the while being careful not to attract any attention at church.

Much to my surprise, he shows up at our home one Sunday

afternoon. We pay no special attention to each other, so my parents suspect nothing. After a few weeks of coming by my family accepts his presence and engage him in conversation about church happenings and life in general.

Both of my parents are out of the house one Sunday afternoon when he pays a visit. We talk and laugh, feeling very comfortable with each other. After a while the others drift away leaving us alone. The conversation becomes intimate, and upon his suggestion we climb the stairs leading to the bedrooms. I sense danger, but allow myself to be reassured that it was okay to be alone in my parent's bedroom with him. Sitting on their bed, he begins caressing and kissing me, telling me how beautiful I am. As the caresses become more intense, I become frightened of impending danger.

"We can't do this," I say, trying to dissuade him. He is ten years my senior and easily convinces me that it will be alright. I get caught up in the fervor of his passion, and before long we are having sex on my parents' bed. This is the first, and only sexual encounter between us.

Chapter Six

SEVENTEEN AND PREGNANT

M y parents return 20 short minutes after Henry leaves. I beg God to conceal from them what had so recently taken place on their bed. I am scared to look them in the face, believing that my sin is absolutely planted on my forehead for them to see. God answers my prayers, because they remain ignorant of my actions. But that answered prayer is short-lived. The second worst thing that could ever happen in my life becomes fact. My gut wrenching agonized cries to God, begging Him to not allow it to be so, go unanswered. But my suspicion becomes real: in two months I realize I am pregnant. Nothing that has happened in my life up to this point – the betrayal of my mother, the rapes, the beatings – has prepared me for the shocking reality of my pregnancy. Never before have I prayed so hard for something not to be. But to my agonizing dismay, it is so, and no amount of praying, wishing, crying, or anything else can save me from certain death. I am 17 and pregnant.

For weeks I hide my morning sickness from the entire household, pretending to gag on something when nausea rises in my throat in the mornings. I wish for death every moment of every day. I tell Henry of my predicament, and he promise to support me in every way. I do not want his support; I want to die.

To my horror, my flat teenage stomach begins to grow. Now I'm really in trouble. How much longer will I be able to conceal this from my parents? I have no confidence in even my father's love. I'm totally alone in this. If a person could cry themselves to death, I would have succumbed to its icy fingers. To make matters worse, Henry decides to tell my parents about the situation. Even after much begging and pleading for him not to carry out his plans, he remains adamant to do the right thing. One evening he shows up at our house. I run upstairs and lock myself in the bedroom, fervently begging God to take my life then and there. He didn't answer my prayer.

With ears glued to the keyhole I listen as my parents are told that I am pregnant. The house is suddenly as still, like the proverbial calm before the storm. My heart leaps into my throat, pounding so hard I hear it in my ears. Trembling in fright, shaking like a leaf, I cry out to God, "God, what is going to become of me?"

Expecting to hear my mother shout my name, I listen, dreading the sound of her voice. Instead, an equally frightened sister knocks on the door, telling me Mama has called for me. She takes one look at me and starts crying. She knows what I already know: Mama is going to kill me.

On wobbly legs and with downcast eyes I enter the room. If looks could kill I would have died on the spot from the venom which spouted from my mother's eyes. I don't know what to do. Should I sit? Stand? Next to whom?

Even Daddy has turned against me: looking at him, the familiar sparkle in his eyes is dimmed by disappointment. I lurk in the back of the room, as far away from everyone as possible.

"Is what I just heard true?" my mother barks at me.

Unable to speak and with eyes fixed on the floor, I nod.

A litany of abuse spews from her mouth. She calls me every name in a truck driver's vocabulary book. I sink lower and lower into the ground. If only some higher being could have mercy on me, causing the ground to open up and swallow me, but that didn't happen either. I have survived a great deal in my 17 years, but not this time. There is no way out of this dilemma.

When Henry gets up to leave, I beg him with my eyes, to stay. At least while he is here, I'm safe from the kicks and punches which I'm sure will come raining down upon my head. Without speaking directly to me, he walks out the door. His eyes speak volumes, but he knows better than to address me. My sisters, feeling my pain and shame, share my discomfort as we watch his retreat. We fear for what will follow. What is she going to do to me? I have brought the ultimate disgrace upon the family.

To everyone's surprise, she didn't touch me, but I wish she would. People say, sticks and stones can break my bones, but words can never hurt me. But her words and actions towards me have broken more than my bones. My spirit, the zeal for life, my ambitions and dreams, everything has been taken away from me, and now I have committed the ultimate unforgivable sin, a sin that in a short time will no longer be a secret. People will begin talking about the family, and worst of all, the church will become involved. What eludes me is that, after all the years of being raped by my godfather, pregnancy had not occurred. Now after just one encounter with someone else, here I am with a child growing deep in my womb.

Mama refuses to speak directly to me, except to curse me every moment that I am in her presence. If we meet in the hallway, she shuffles back, holding her dress away from me in an effort to avoid contracting my leprosy. I am forbidden to have meals at the table with the family, and become an outcast in the household. None of what I have experienced before was as painful as this loathing. I know I have done wrong, but does she have to treat me with such scorn and disdain?

Daddy, after his initial shock and disappointment, tries to make me feel comfortable. They fight day and night over me, and I cry constantly. As my stomach grows, so does mother's hatred of me. My sisters suffer right along with me, as they bear the brunt of her anger. I am hopeless and helpless, unable to withstand anymore.

To make the entire situation worse, there is one huge disgraceful, insurmountable problem: Henry is married.

The ultimate disgrace takes place two weeks later. My parents are not home. Startled by a loud bang and raised voices, we rush to the front door. Peering out the window we see to our horror Mavis, Henry's wife, accompanied by her mother, sister and brother. Metals clash as they bang on the gate with an iron pipe, yelling my name, daring me to come out so she could rip her husband's child out of me after killing me.

"Come out here, Marcia McLaren, you little whore! Come out so I can kick your ass! I want a piece of you! If you think you are a woman, come out that door!"

O God, no. Not this, anything but this. He had promised not to tell her about the pregnancy. Has he broken his promise the same way he promised that I would be safe?

"Little bitch, you and that pickney will never be safe. I promise to kill both of you. Wherever you go for the rest of your life, you had better look over your shoulders, because if it's one day before I die, I will kill you."

"God, why can't you just kill me now?" I silently pray. "This can not be happening. I'll never be able to live this down. Please, I am guilty as charged. Please execute judgment against me and kill me now."

Her mother, sister and brother add their threats to hers.

Bang, bang on the gate with a length of iron. The cussing, name-calling and threats continue for about an hour.

I'm mortified, killed by shame. We're prisoners, fortressing ourselves behind the iron bars of the grilled gate and locked door. With every clang on the gate my distress grows. The barking dogs in the yard and jeers of the neighbors who gather to enjoy the free show kill everything in me that has not already succumbed. Again, I beg God to rescue me by taking my life. How can I walk the streets again?

After satisfying themselves by calling me every conceivable name and bringing the neighborhood to the gate to glare, they walk away sneering and laughing, leaving me shaken, intimidated, and scared for my life. I'm too ashamed to ever walk out the door again.

"What happened to the gate, why is it all bent and twisted?" Mama asks as she tries to open it to come into the yard. It takes the strength of four to release the lock.

"What happened here?" she asks again.

None of us want to be the bearer of bad news, so no one speaks.

"Marcia, what happened to the gate? I want an answer now."

With head hung low I explain that Mavis had come to the house, cursing and hitting the gate with a piece of iron.

"See what you have brought upon the family? Look at the disgrace you have caused, having a woman come to my gate to cuss you because you are carrying her husband's child. If I was here, I would have opened the door and pushed you outside so she could beat you to death. Right now, death is the best thing that could happen to you. How am I supposed to hold my head up in the neighborhood after this? Get out of my sight you disgusting thing! You make me sick!"

Not as sick as I am. When will this come to an end? Finding the darkest corner in the house, I huddle there, stroking my bulging stomach.

My baby seems to sense the turmoil swirling around me, and I whisper to her, "I don't know what's going to happen to us, sweetheart. Now I am scared to walk the streets because Mavis threatens to be behind every corner, waiting for an opportunity to kill us. I don't know what to do. But I will give my life to protect you. It's you and me against the world, my love."

After a particularly hard night of listening to Mama's hate and disgust at the sight of me, I tearfully informed my godfather of the situation at home. I'm desperate, and cannot continue living like this. I ask for his permission to move into his home for a while. He says yes, at least until the tension at home calms down. I know that this was not going to be a good situation; but my decision is made based on the lesser of the two evils. I have endured enough from Mama. Living conditions have become unbearable, my emotions are raw, and conflict is high. My mother hates the sight of me and the household is suffering because of me. My condition is a disgraceful evidence of my sin, in full view for all to see. They are all ashamed of me. I have to go.

Returning home from work that evening I tell the chauffeur to wait for me, as I will be returning to the home with him.

I tell Mama of my decision to leave the home, to which she promptly replies, "Good riddance! Don't bother coming back with your bastard pickney, and I hope Nowington kicks you out, too, because you'll be a disgrace and embarrassment to him."

Daddy is not home, but he will be told when he comes home. My sisters cry at my departure, and my heart breaks with distress, but this has to be done. I can no longer live under the same roof with my mother in my present state.

Taking up residence at my godfather's, is similar to making my bed in hell. On the first night of my arrival, the sexual abuse, which had abated, begins again. My pregnancy means nothing to him, and now that I'm completely at his mercy, totally dependent upon him for a salary, shelter and for food. It's almost worse than living at home. But the die has been cast: my decision has been made. Now I had to deal with it. With gritted teeth and tears rolling down my cheeks, I endure him having his way with me nightly. I tell Henry where I am and he comes to visit. I'm careful not to mention the nightly assaults, and convince him that I'm safe. He calls frequently, and assists with preparations for our baby's arrival.

The church has heard about my pregnancy, and instead of doing what I mistakenly think is the right thing – to help a sinner who has fallen from grace to find her way back – a church board meeting is called, and the decision is made that Henry and I will be excommunicated from the church. We will no longer be members of the denomination. This decision hurt almost as much as my mother's words. I cry my heart out. These people, who the Lord had admonished to "Feed my sheep," have just banished two sheep from the fold because they have fallen. I feel as if the last straw to which I am clinging to for dear life – the last place where I think God can be found – has been yanked away from me.

I did not expect them to welcome me with open arms, but at least a visit from the pastor to talk about the situation may have helped my feeling of desolation. I have not only been severed from my parents and family, but also from church, and from God. If this is the way church members are treated when they need the support of this extended family, then I want nothing more to do with them, nor, for that matter, with their God. My mother has already tarnished any misconceptions I may have had about a good God who cares for His children, and now the church has administered the final blow. I have truly become an outcast.

My life continues to be a living nightmare from which I cannot awaken. A trial had taken place, the jury has come in, and I have been sentenced to life in hell. There is little contact with my sisters, there are no friends to talk with, and neither of my parents bother visiting me. My days are spent working, and nights are spent being raped. Crying because of the pain doesn't matter. Crying in despair doesn't help. Begging God to rescue me by way of death isn't working, either. No one responds to my pleas. I'm helpless and no one cares enough about me to help, or protect my baby or me.

One night, I'm exceptionally tired of the unwanted sexual advances. I lock myself in the bedroom, hoping to keep him away. Lying there in fear, I don't know how he's going to react, but hope the locked door will dissuade his advances. When he tries the door finding it locked, he knocks. He calls my name, but I refuse to respond. He knocks again calling me again. I continue to feign sleep. I'm determined not to let him in. To my horror, he delivers a few kicks to the door, kicking it right off the hinges. In fury, he enters the room, wearing nothing but his underpants. Nervously I sit up in bed pulling the covers up to my chin.

"This is my house, and everything and everyone in it belongs to me, to be used by me whenever I please. If you do not want to follow my rules, then pack your bags and get out. But as long as you live here you will be available to me whenever I choose to have you. Do you understand that?"

Not waiting for an answer, he roughly pushes me down on the bed and satisfies himself as I bawl.

I am delirious with distress and agonize daily about my situation. Where am I going to put my baby when she is born? The due date is fast approaching. It's to the point where my days are barely tolerable. I place one foot in front of the other; perform my duties, smiling accordingly. My heart has been torn to shreds, and I'm miserable beyond words. At nights, after he's finished with me, I hug my growing belly and apologize to my unborn child. My only friend and companion was this little life growing inside of me. I hope it's a girl. I call her my little baby girl.

"It's just you and me against the world, my precious little baby girl, just you and me against the world."

I repeat this phrase to her nightly, growing strength from the fact that I must protect her against the world.

As she moves within me, my heart comes back to life. I fall in love. I love her unconditionally. I keep apologizing to my baby for putting both of us at the mercy of the two people who have hurt me most in my life, but promise that somehow we will manage to rise above my present situation. One day I will be able to provide for my baby, independent of them. I promise myself that if anyone ever tries to hurt or harm my baby, I will go to prison for murder.

The months pass and my delivery date is dangerously close. Passing each other on the steps one afternoon, my godfather, just as coldly as he had raped me, tells me that I could no longer remain at his home because I have become a source of embarrassment to him. My steps falter, I hold onto the wall for support as my head swims from his words.

"Where am I supposed to go?" I ask him.

"I'm going to call your parents and tell them to come and take you home," He replies. "It's no longer appropriate for you to remain here."

I'm seven and one half months pregnant. I lock myself in the room and cry and cry and cry. Why couldn't God have mercy on me and deliver me from this for good? What am I going to do now? There is no way I'm returning home to the scorn and verbal abuse of my mother. I would rather die first.

But death did not visit me that night. Two evenings later, my parents arrive. I'm shocked to see them, as no one had bothered to tell me that they were coming. I promptly hide myself in my room. They have not seen me in months and I cannot face them.

They talk for a while, and suddenly there's a knock on the door that startles me. Before I can answer, it opens and my angry mother enters the room.

"Look at you," she spits in contempt. "A total disgrace and a big failure. Everybody had such high hopes for you, and look at you: breeding for a married man at 17. You are a disgrace to the family and to your godfather. I don't want you back in my house, and your godfather doesn't want you here any longer, so what are you going to do now?"

With my face turned to the wall and eyes almost swollen shut from crying, I frantically try to figure out what to do. I give serious consideration to getting one of his guns (he keeps two in his room) and shooting myself. But what if I succeed in killing myself, but my baby survives? What will become of her? No, regardless of what happens to me, I have to remain alive for her sake. To protect her from my mother and my godfather, I will survive this at any cost.

After telling me how much she despises me, she leaves the room and I cry some more. My father, who I thought loved me so much, does not bother looking at or speaking to me. I guess he is too ashamed of me to look me in my face. A household help come to tell me to pack my belongings and go home with my parents. In astonishment I look at her.

"I'm not going." I said.

"Miss Marcia they told me to tell you to get ready."

"I don't care what they say. I am not going"

She leaves the room shaking her head. I lock it and bawl loudly not caring who hears me. No, no, no! I was not returning home with them. I will rather become homeless.

They hear the disturbance and my mother returns to the door. "Open the door," she orders.

"No!"

I continue screaming. No amount of talking can get me to move. He will have to kick the door in again. They try talking to me from the other side of the door, and I stubbornly refuse to budge. Finally they leave me alone and return home. My godfather also leaves me alone that night.

But my reprieve is short-lived. The following day, while I work in the office, unknown to me, he orders the help to pack my belongings and have the chauffeur place them in the car trunk. When I return to my room at the end of the work day, it's empty of my things.

"What happened to my stuff?" I ask the help who's walking with me along the hallway.

"I'm sorry Miss Marcia, but Mr. Nowington told me to pack them up and put them in the car so the chauffeur can take you home."

I'm dumbfounded. How can he do this to me?

I lock myself in the bathroom crying. Minutes later when I come out, he is calmly leaning against the wall with arms folded across his chest waiting for me.

"You have to go home. The car is waiting for you and the chauffeur has to go home, so hurry up. It's close to your due date and I can't keep you here any longer. Don't worry about work. We'll manage without you until after the baby is born. I'll send you your salary as usual. Your job will be here when you are ready to come back. Now go and take care of yourself. Good-bye."

With those words I'm escorted out the door and into the waiting car.

Chapter Seven

SURVIVAL

Up to this point in my life, I thought I had lived through hell. But the reality is that what has happened before was only a taste of how cruel my mother really can be. Compared to the treatment meted out to me upon my return home, I had been a cherished child before. Of course, I did not expect to be greeted with open arms and a "Welcome Home" banner across the front porch – after all, I had done wrong and broken all the rules, bringing unwanted scrutiny and shame upon the family. I'm a disappointment and an embarrassment to my parents and to my siblings, who have to answer unwanted questions about my condition. The church members treat them nearly as badly as they treated me, almost to the point of holding them responsible for my actions.

The neighbors look on with curiosity, waiting to see what will happen to the pregnant teenage daughter of this home, where the children had not been allowed to mingle with their children because our mother behaved as if we are better than them. Little do they know that we are the most ill-treated and abused children in the entire neighborhood.

The drive home seems too short. I do not have enough time to sort out my thoughts, to devise a plan of action, to think about the sudden change of circumstances. This could not be happening. The night before, I was unable to even face them. How am I going to live with them? My stomach is huge, so there is no disguising my situation. My baby moves within me, and tears instantly spring to my eyes. It's as if she senses the tension and uncertainty, and is trying to reach out and reassur me that everything is going to be okay. But was it really going to be okay? Will we survive my mother?

How am I going to protect my baby?

With butterflies in my stomach, trembling hands, and tears in my eyes, I sit silently in the car, willing the chauffeur to continue driving. But he stops the car, looks back at me, and announces that we are here. He walks to my side of the car and opens the door for me to leave the safety of the vehicle. Slowly, I shuffle my body to the door, trying to prolong the inevitable for just a few more seconds. One of my sisters notices the car at the gate with me sitting in it. Excitedly she cries my name, running out to greet me. She takes a long look at my swollen stomach and hugs me telling me how much she had missed me. Mother, hearing the voices, comes to see what's going on.

Her eyes narrow into slits and her hands go akimbo. I'm scared to venture into the gate, but my suitcases have been removed from the car trunk and the chauffer is carrying them through the gate. My sister softly encourages me to come on. She senses the fear and my hesitation as my steps falter and my head goes down.

"She can't do anything to you," my sister whispers in my ear, but in my heart I know better. Mama can do a lot to me and to my unborn baby. At this moment I'm more scared of her than I have ever been in my life.

Timidly I walk toward the door. She watches me without saying a word. I approach the steps. She flings her arms down in exasperation, spits in the grass, and whirls around, huffing away. I'm crushed. Nothing has changed in the five months I have been away. My father and other siblings are happy to have me back. To make my life a little easier, Daddy says that I can have a newly added room to the house, so my baby's crying will not disturb the family at nights. I like this arrangement, and am thankful for small mercies. Henry had bought a crib and other baby items, which are already in the room.

Is it possible for a seven-and-one-half-months pregnant teenager to remain invisible? I have to find a way to do just that. I learn to stay out of my mother's way. I observe her movements and move around only when she is out of the house or in another part of it. Her scorn of me is so great that if our paths cross at the same point, she hastily reverses her steps, walking in another direction. When she has no choice but to speak to me, she does so in the harshest tone possible. I am constantly reminded of how awful I look, the failure and disappointment I am, and the disgrace I have brought upon the household.

She hates the sight of me, and I try blending into the furniture to avoid her scrutiny. This is impossible. One day she hears me telling one of my sisters to put her hand on my stomach to feel the baby's movements. She quickly puts a stop to that, accusing me of encouraging my sisters to follow me in my lewd and disgraceful behavior. She takes no part in the preparation for the baby, but we are able to acquire all the necessary items. In her absence we lovingly wash, fold and pack away the tiny garments, daydreaming about my baby's arrival which is only days away.

Amelia and Victoria hear about the situation and visit us from Canada. We are delighted to see them. They encourage me and talk to mother about her harsh treatment of me. This only makes the situation worse. They tell me I'm the first child to become pregnant while living in the home, and give me credit for surviving her venom. While shampooing my hair one morning, Amelia notices the color of my ear wax. "Marcia why is the wax in your ear white?"

"I don't know. I know that it is white but I have been thinking when you are pregnant you have white wax."

"Child stop your foolishness, pregnancy has nothing to do with the color of your ear wax. Has your ear been hurting you?"

"Yes, it hurts and it's itchy."

"You have an ear infection, and it's pus that's coming out of your ear, I'm surprised that you can still hear. You need to go to the doctor."

I go to the doctor, he examines my ear canal and prescribes antibiotics and ear drops. It takes months for the infection to be cured, leaving me with a perforated ear drum.

Before returning to Canada, my sisters give me their contact information.

My baby will soon be born. I have to stop worrying about my survival and focus on the life of my innocent child about to be born into this dysfunctional family. Regardless of the cost, this child will be protected and loved and cared for. She will be kept out of the clutches of the evil that have been a part of my life.

Daddy is silent during this entire episode. He disapproves of my behavior, is disappointed about what has happened, but he is never cruel to me. He speaks to me in normal tones and tries to help me bear the wrath of Mama. Secretly, he slips me money to help prepare for the baby and even asks how I feel. He has to be careful not to be caught showing any attention to me, or he will be accused of condoning my behavior. Nevertheless he endures hell from her, especially at nights when she thinks we're asleep.

"I was right," I overhear her say to Daddy one night, "All that money we wasted on sending her to school could have been put to better use. See, she ended up as nothing, just as I predicted."

"The child made a mistake. That does not mean she is worthless."

"She is worthless – no better than a dog. I hate the sigh of her. I should have taken a coat hanger to her, ripping the bastard pickney out of her so I wouldn't have to look at her now."

"You are crazy. She is not the first person to get pregnant. Give her a chance. I'm sure she'll make something out of her life later. Don't be so hard on her. All I ever see her do is cry. She is sorry for what happened."

"Take up for her all you want. If you were a better father this would not have happened, but you always defend them so they think they can do whatever they want and get away with it. Well not this time. As soon as she pushes out that baby, she had better find somewhere else to live. I'm not having them live in here with me."

"Where do you expect her to go?"

"I don't give a damn, just as long as she is out of my sight."

Daddy defends me. But his defense is useless.

I cover my mouth with my hands in an attempt to stifle the agonizing cries, which rise in my throat. Those words burn a hole as deep as the Grand Canyon in my soul. I purpose in my heart, silently

78

promising Daddy and myself. "Don't worry Daddy, I promise that if it's one day before death's icy fingers claim me from this world, I will become somebody. Her prediction has to be proven wrong. If it takes my entire life I will show her that I am worth something. Thank you for trying to take up for me."

I'm almost ready to give birth and am very uncomfortable. On my last doctors visit, Henry meets me at the doctor's office (he has been forbidden to visit me at home). He promises to visit me in the hospital, willing to disregard my mother's orders to stay away from me. He wants to see his child. I do not know what to expect in the delivery room and I am scared, but I'm ready to deliver my baby. Maybe if my mother is not constantly reminded of what I had done each time she lays eyes on me my life may be a little easier. But then again, whoever said life is easy?

During the twilight hours of Monday morning, September 16th, the pain in my stomach awakens me. After I sit up in bed for a few minutes, they subside. I try returning to sleep and almost succeed when another sharp pain has me hugging my stomach, swaying back and forth, moaning. I don't know what to do, and I'm certainly not going to wake my mother. I try to make myself comfortable, nodding off when I can, rolling around groaning softly when the pain returns. At daybreak I take a shower, returning to my bed as I wait for the household to come awake for the day. By this time I realize that I'm in labor, with contractions about fifteen minutes apart.

One of my sisters is the first to come downstairs and enter my room to check on me. I tell her what has been happening and she gets my parents. A barrage of questions: how long have you been in pain? Why didn't you wake us? How bad is it? While the questions are coming, a contraction comes right along and everyone springs into action. We must get to the hospital. My sisters want to accompany us to the hospital, but they are told no; they have to go to school. I'm helped into clothing, my packed bag retrieved, and a taxi is called. In silence I sit next to my father as we drive to the hospital. When the contractions come, I silently squeeze his hand, gritting my teeth, biting my lips to keep from screaming. I have resolved one thing in my heart. If it kills me, I am not going to cry in my mother's presence. I do not care how terrible the pain is, she is not going to hear me cry to give her the satisfaction of telling me that I should have thought of this before doing what I had done. I'm not going to cry.

Not only do I want to cry, I want to scream, I want to throw my head back, and allow the pain which swells up in my body, exploding somewhere in my inner parts, to be expelled through my throat. I want to throw my legs apart and beg somebody, anybody to please rid my body of this child, which was causing such unbelievable red-hot searing pain to rip through my body. I want somebody to hold me and tell me it's going to be over soon. Somebody to tell me they love me, encourage me to hang in there just a little longer. But there is no one. Not a sound is uttered, except for a moan as I allow my head to roll back swallowing what rises up in me. No sir, I'm not going to cry in her presence. Not even if it kills me.

The taxi driver senses that he has to hurry. He careens through the morning traffic, hitting every pothole on the street of Kingston. Every hole brings a fresh wave of pain, but with some unseen help I stick to my resolve. We arrive at the hospital, I'm assisted out of the car into a wheelchair. My parents follow the nurse as she wheels me in to be registered. The pre-delivery preparation is completed. I'm in agony with contractions ten minutes apart.

In a few minutes, they have me admitted and in a bed in the delivery room. At last I can succumb to the pain, which seems to have no end. A nurse comes in to check my vital signs, and as if on cue, my water breaks. I'm embarrassed, but she quickly puts me at ease. She gets help changing the bed linens, making me as comfortable as possible. My baby is about to be born. The pain is agonizing. Our future is uncertain, but I'm not going to worry about it now. I give myself over to what is happening, allowing this experience to take place. When this is over will we be all right?

What is going to become of us?

I have no idea.

Chapter Eight

MY FIRST BORN

Monday, September 16, 1975 seems to have no end. The day is spent in agony, first in the taxi, then thrashing around in a hospital bed with no comforting voice of love next to me. There is no one there offering a hand for me to squeeze, no one to wipe the sweat of labor from my forehead, assuring me it would be over soon. Alone, I cry, trying to find the strength to hang in there to give birth to my baby. I have no idea of the whereabouts of my parents and don't even care; I only know that I'm alone and in unbearable pain. As the day wears on I receive medication that helps me to relax, and even lulls me into a restless sleep, which last for a few minutes. The nurses and doctor keep a constant watch on me, commenting that I'm young and small and teenage mothers giving birth for the first time usually takes longer. I find no comfort in those words; I only want to get it over and done with. But I'm powerless to speed up the process.

Exactly one month and 15 days earlier, I had turned 18, and should have been in college somewhere or in an office working at making a living and planning how to get out of my mother's house. Instead of planning a party to celebrate the beginning of adulthood, I'm in a hospital room waiting to give birth to a baby. This is not what I wanted, and not what I planned or hoped for during my teenage years, but it happened, and regardless of what anyone else says, this baby is going to be very special to me. She (I'm hoping for a girl) is going to receive so much love from me that she will not miss the love of a father or of anyone else that choose not to love her. I will love her enough for the entire world.

The pain becomes unbearable, with the contractions only a couple minutes apart. The medical team gets active, monitoring my progress. I'm transferred from one bed to another, crying out in the pain of being moved. Almost immediately my body feels as if it's being ripped into a million pieces. The nurses get me ready in the birthing position, telling me not to push until they tell me to. (I still wonder how they expect a woman in the throes of labor not to push). I try to follow the instructions, but my body wants to do otherwise. My young body begs for release as I scream with every push. The life inside fights desperately to be released from the confines of her embryonic sac, longing for the umbilical cord to be cut so she can breathe on her own for the first time.

The doctor and nurses try coaching me along. They announce she is coming, "her head is crowned." I have no idea what that means. The pressure to push is so great that I'm unable to control the urge; with every ounce of strength left in me I give a huge push, experiencing instant relief, as they announce.

"It's a girl."

Instantly I forget about the last 18 hours of agony. My little baby girl has been born. As they clean her up, I try to get a glimpse of my daughter, but they still have work for me to do. I have to wait a few more minutes to see her. As soon as they are finished with the details, they ease me into a sitting position, and gently put my baby in my arms.

It's the happiest day of my life. Cradling my baby, looking into her beautiful face, a fresh wave of tears washes over me. This time they are tears of joy. Checking to see if she has ten fingers and ten toes, I hold her close to my heart, kissing her. A love I did not know could exist flows through me. My heart races with love for her from every fiber of my being. I know that only death will be able to separate us. I love her enough to fight the world for her, and if necessary give my life for her. I love her with an everlasting love, a love that knows no end. In those first moments of meeting my daughter for the first time, I know that there is nothing I will not do for her.

I can't get enough of her. Quietly she sleeps in my arms. The nurse comes in to take her to the nursery.

"No," I protested, "please let me keep her with me."

"You have to get your rest." She tells me. "You just did a great deal of work and need to recover. Don't worry, we'll bring her back later. Now get some rest."

I relinquish her, following the retreating nurse with my eyes through the door. Not realizing how exhausted I am, I stretch out on the bed and fall asleep.

I awake to the sound of voices. A porter tells me that he's moving me to another room, and that it is visiting time. A few minutes later, my baby is brought to me. I'm told to put her to my breast for her to begin getting used to sucking. She latches on to my breast and I get the biggest thrill out of the experience. My own little baby has arrived, and is now totally dependent upon me for sustenance. Will I be able to provide for her?

What an angel she is, absolutely beautiful, perfect in every way. Her skin is of the finest velvet, her face as smooth and beautiful as the rising sun. Her big black eyes are like the morning stars shining in all their glory. Her cheeks have been kissed by God himself and she glows from the encounter. She smells like the aroma from the most expensive perfume house in France. All seven and a half pounds and 21 inches make her, without a doubt, the most beautiful baby to ever have been born into this world. I love her with all my heart.

Visiting hours begin and in come my parents. For the first time in my life, I do not care what my mother thinks or says. Nothing she says today is going to have any effect on me. They ask how I am as they examine my baby. I wonder if my mother expects her to have two heads and one eye. Cautiously she pulls back the blanket, peeking at her. I watch her face for a negative reaction, and I'm stunned into silence when she announces that she is a beautiful baby. Inwardly, I smile. She is beautiful, but I know better than to agree with my mother. Moments later, Henry arrives. He enters the room, looks around, and heads directly for my bed. I want to proudly display our baby, but my mother is present, watching my every move, so I calmly hand his daughter to him. He takes one look at her and the biggest smile I had ever seen covers his face

"What a beautiful little girl."

He kisses her, holding her close. He is proud of his daughter.

Our hospital stay lasts for two days. My parents do not return the second day, but Henry does. Without their presence, he sits and we talk. I have never told him about the hardships I endured during the pregnancy, nor about any of the abuse by my mother and godfather. He asks if I had been okay, and I simply reply, "I'm fine." This is probably a mistake – maybe if I had told him about the situation at home, he would provide a home for us, but I'm confused and ashamed of my life. I feel that telling him may drive him away, so I keep my mouth shut. I don't know what we're going home to. But whatever happens, somehow we will survive.

On the third day of her birth we are discharged from the hospital. The hospital porter wheels us through the front door. There is no one waiting to take us home.

"Who is going to pick you up?" He asks.

"No one" I replied.

"Would you like me to get you a taxi?" He asks.

"Yes," I replied.

He hails a taxi; we're bundled into it and the journey of uncertainty begins. I arrive at my parents' home, but there is no one there. I have neither a key or money. What am I going to do?"

A neighbor looks out, noticing my predicament. She offers to pay the taxi driver and invites me to wait on her porch for someone to come home. Gladly I accept the offer, sitting down while the family looks at my baby, all exclaiming how beautiful she is. Shortly afterwards my mother arrives home. My suitcase is sitting inside the gate. She notices it. Knowing no one is homes she looks around for me. She sees me sitting on the neighbor's porch. I begin gathering my baby's blanket around her to go home. She is furious. I cross the street. She lashes out at me.

"What make you so proud of your bastard pickney that as soon as you get home you have to go to people's house to show it off?"

"I'm not showing her off." I tried explaining. "But there was no one home and I don't have a key, so she offered me a seat on her porch until someone came home."

"You should just sit down on the steps over here. You have nothing to be proud of."

Blinking back tears, I suck in my hurt feelings. I hug my baby a little tighter, saying not one more word.

"Look at you," she continues. "a baby in your arms and no husband at your side. Your father and I have to take on this responsibility, as if we don't have enough mouths to feed. Get inside. I hate the very sight of you."

Things are going to be tough, life is going to be difficult…but somehow, somehow we will make it.

What I have failed to understand is my mother's animosity and berating of me because I'm unmarried. I know Henry is married and I'm ashamed of that. For a long time, she refers to my baby as a bastard. Has she forgotten that it was her doing that introduced me to sex at the young age of 12? Has she forgotten that all five children born to her and Daddy had been conceived and born out of wedlock? Has she forgotten that she is no paragon of virtue? Has she forgotten about the mercies and forgiveness of God?

Thankfully, the rest of the family arrives home soon. My sisters are ecstatic and welcome their niece into the family. From that day forward, my baby, whom I named Jessica Anita, becomes the love of everyone's life. She is a sweetheart of a baby, crying only when her needs are to be met. In no time she is laughing and playing, winning every heart in the household. Even mother falls in love with her. Her personality is infectious; she is pure joy to behold. Her father visits often, delighting in her. As soon as she is old enough to sit up he puts her on his shoulders taking her for walks throughout the neighborhood. My Daddy loves her, and gets immense pleasure from bouncing her on his knees. Life at home becomes a little easier.

Mama and I clash often, as we now disagree over the rearing of my child. I will be dammed if I'm going to allow her to have any significant input in Jessica's life. We live in her home but I'm determined to raise my child without her influence.

Jessica is six months old. Mother informs me that the church board has decided that Henry and I are eligible for rebaptism since there has been no evidence that we have continued having a relationship. The event will take place two weeks later. I have no interest in being rebaptized or resuming church attendance. I harbor no desire to become a new spectacle, or the new topic of gossip, but mother tells me that if I do not comply with the decision of the church I cannot continue living under her roof. Two weeks later I dutifully show up at church and we're both dipped into the pool. I guess by this action they have rewritten my name on the church roll, giving God permission to re-admit me into heaven. The truth is I hate the entire bunch of them. I hate my mother, I hate the church and I hate the church members.

Now that I had been cleansed of my sins, my baby can be "blessed" in the holy sanctuary. The date is set for next Sabbath. I refuse to attend the service. On Sabbath morning my parents take Jessica to church while I remained home, fuming about all the hypocrites who will be feigning happiness for us, making their snide remarks, admiring her only to have our names as the main course over Sabbath lunch.

Breaking under pressure from mother, I attend church the following week. The stares and whisperings are so long, loud and scornful that, after a few weeks, I refuse to resume regular attendance. The atmosphere is just too uncomfortable. I don't care what my mother says; I'm not going back. Daddy tells her to leave me alone, but she tells him to stay out of it.

At her insistence and threats to kick me out of the house if I don't comply, I accompany them to church another Sabbath morning. Entering the property, I can't believe my eyes. My steps falter, coming to a halt. There, right smack in the front yard, surrounded by a full entourage and leading the family into battle, is Mavis, with her mother, sisters and brother at her side. How did they know that I would be here today? Fear grips my heart. I clutch Jessica to my chest, refusing to proceed further.

She notices us. Mavis breaks away from her gang coming directly at me. She bellows obscenities, threatening to kill us on the spot. Daddy places his arms around me. Mother glares at me yelling, "You are never going to stop being a disgrace to this family. Are you? Now I can't even go to church in peace. Why can't you just die? If she wants to beat you right here you deserve it. Get the hell away from me."

Mavis is in my face, cursing and threatening me with death. Daddy defends me. "To get to her you are going to have to go through me. Leave her alone. What is done is done, so stop harassing her. She made a mistake. As a matter of fact, your husband is the adult in this mess. He is a married man who should have known better. Have you asked him what was he doing with my 17-year-old daughter? You need to deal with him. She is trying to go on with her life. Leave my daughter alone."

Tears run down my face, dropping onto my sleeping baby's blanket. With a few choice words, Mavis turn on her heels returning to the churchyard fuming, and cursing, protesting my presence at the top of her voice. Slowly, we bring up the rear as the deacons and members come out to see what the commotion is about. I just want to get away, but my mother forbids me to leave.

"You brought this upon yourself. Now deal with the consequences. For the rest of your life you'll have to hide from her, so get used to it. I have to put up with these indignations and insults. Everyone is talking about me behind my back, all because of you. Now go find a seat in church."

"That's why I didn't want to come. You made me. Why can't I go home?'

"Shut up and go inside. It's your fault and your disgrace. Deal with it."

Finding a seat in the back, I perch on the edge of the bench. My eyes never stop scanning every direction. The enemy is on the same property. We are in danger. My fears are not unfounded. Shortly after I sit down, the pack comes charging around the corner in search of their prey. Hunching low, I ease myself, with my baby in my arms into the farthest corner. Their eyes scan the congregation for a glimpse of me. They are out for my blood.

Like the children of Israel marching around the city of Jericho to topple it, so the clan storms around the building looking for me. The elders and deacons try their best to restore peace to the scared grounds, but it's useless. The pastor takes control of the situation, herding them all into his office while I hide in the back. They charge out of his office yelling insults at the minister.

"I have every right to be here! She should not be allowed on the property. What type of church are you running harboring the likes of her? We are not leaving. Find her and make her leave. She is the slut."

Mavis has been trying to get her hands on me, and now she has me in sight. She smells my blood in her nostrils and is not giving up.

I'm scared to death. A deacon notices me, and quietly ushers me into the office.

"Be quiet," he admonishes. "If she can't find you she'll eventually leave."

My life flashes before my eyes. I have no hope. How can I live like this? I'll never be safe again. Holding my baby tightly, I beg God to strike us both dead, to release the innocent little angel I am holding from this mess.

"Lord, I can't go on. I am scared, embarrassed and petrified. My family is suffering because of me. My mother hates me even more, if that's possible. Please have mercy on us and take our lives now, I'll never be able to live a normal life. My baby will grow up with this stigma on her. She doesn't deserve it. She has done nothing wrong. Help us, Lord. Help us out of this."

But He doesn't answer me. The service has been disrupted with everyone enjoying a free show. They snicker and laugh, talking about me, taking sides with Mavis and her family. I am the enemy of the entire congregation. I brought sin and its repercussions into their midst. I am doomed. The din outside subsides. Slowly the door opens and the deacon enters. With a sympathetic look on his face, he says.

"It's safe now. They left."

"No, I am too ashamed. Everyone is talking about me. I can't face them."

"Okay. Stay here until the service ends, I'll tell your family where you are."

"Thank you."

At the end of the worship service I leave the room on wobbly legs, with down cast eyes and tear-streaked face. Baby in arms, I walk away from the New Haven SDA church. I will never return.

I purpose in my heart that if there is a God who loves and cares for me and my baby, He will have to find a way to convince me to come back to Him. He will have to give me a reason to go back to church. God Himself will have to appear to me to make me want anything to do with the things pertaining to Him. From this point on, I begin living my life without giving any thought to God.

☙

Chapter Nine

UNCONSENTED ABORTION

Returning to work three months later means leaving my baby in the care of my mother. This is not my first choice but, for a fee, she decides that no one can do a better job of caring for her grandchild than she can. Against my better judgment, I agree to the plan, thinking that since Jessica is a baby there is not much harm that can be inflicted upon her. Mother knows better than to physically abuse her. Daily when I get home from work, I scrutinize Jessica's entire body looking for marks or bruises.

Jessica grows into a beautiful, intelligent little girl. At four months, she begins teething. At seven months, she takes her first step, and says her first words at eleven months. She has truly become a blessing in the home. Even mother dotes on her. My life is now centered on her. Everything I do is done with her welfare in mind. I'm accused of spoiling her. I certainly spoil her, but so does everyone else. I want to leave my parents home and provide for both of us on my own, but I'm not making enough money to be independent yet. So, I continue living here, working for my godfather and saving what I can.

I have had no relationship of any type with a man, so when Jessica turns one year old and I become pregnant again, I know who has to be the father. After returning to work, things are good for a while. He leaves me alone for a couple months. Then it's election time and we have to travel to the parish he represents in the Island. The trip requires us to spend five days out of town. As his personal assistant,

I have to accompany the team on the trip. It's distressing leaving my baby, but I trust my sisters to take care of her for me. The obligations of the job have to be met, and for the first time in her life, I have to leave my baby for five days.

At the end of the first day in St. Thomas, we all retire to bed. Thinking I'm safe in my room, I neglect to lock the door and am awaken to the presence of someone getting into bed with me. I try jumping off the bed, but he is poised above me, pinning me to the bed. I thrash around, kicking my legs, trying to escape his clutches. He holds me in a tight grip, refusing to release my arm. I beg him not to do what I know he intends to do. I begin crying, begging him to stop, but he simply ignores my pleas and like old times, he rapes me.

I spend the rest of the night crying. I'm back to square one. For a while, I had began to feel like a normal human being, but those feelings have been dashed. My godfather had only been waiting for the right opportunity to assault me again. I'm a little older now, have given birth to a baby, and although I am still vulnerable to him and am still subjected to my mother's rules, I am stronger and will no longer silently succumb to them. The following night, I try to lock the door and find that the lock doesn't work. I suspect it have been tampered with, making it impossible to keep him out. Of course he comes in and rapes me again. During the next day, I secretly ask the maintenance man to take a look at the lock and fix the problem. He obliges. I still worry though, because a little thing like a lock has failed to keep my godfather at bay before.

The third night I carefully lock the door. A little later I hear him trying to enter the room, but find the door locked. He curses under his breath and goes back to his room. I prop a chair under the doorknob, trying to make sure I'm safe for the night. I drift off into restless sleep filled with nightmares. Work the next day is strained. I am red eyed from crying and try avoiding him, except when it's necessary for work.

Others join us the fourth day with a few of them deciding to spend the night there after working late into the night. When the meeting finally breaks up and we separate to retire for the night, I discover that a new arrival have been given my room. I ask the help why and where am I supposed to sleep? She tells me that Mr.

Nowington told her to give my room to the guest. I therefore need to speak with him. He is still entertaining a few male guests, so I sit down in a corner reading a book while I wait. He excuses himself from the group to visit the restroom and I confront him

"Uncle Nowington, Gina tells me that you told her to give my room to a guest. All the other rooms are full. Where am I supposed to sleep?"

With a sinister smile he replies.

"You will be sleeping with me tonight, so go get ready and wait for me in bed until I come in." I'm in shock. How low will he go?

This man is a leader in the community, is a minister in the country's government, whom everyone looks up to. People thinks he is a good man, helping them to get their lives together, providing jobs for the people, making laws which affect the lives of the entire nation. He is a person with enormous power, and great wealth, who can with the stroke of a pen or one telephone call, change lives for the better or worse. He is a tyrant, a rapist and a horrible individual who wields his power over everyone. He is used to getting whatever and whomever he wants.

He is also a person who is once again trying to convince the people to vote for him, to give him another five years at the helm of the country, to work and provide stability for them. This same man had viciously raped me at the age of 12 and for several years after.

This man of power, who is my godfather, has devised a plan to make me available to him. Not risking the chance that I will lock the door against him again, he leaves me with no place to sleep except in his bed, so he can have his way with me all night. Well he is not going to have his way tonight. I'm no longer going to silently lie down and allow him to violate me anymore. I'm going to fight for myself. If he fires me then, so be it. He has taken advantage of me for so long, that it has become a way of life for him. I decide that if he forces himself upon me one more timef I'm going to reveal his true nature to someone. I am going to tell the wife of one of our founding fathers of the political party which he represented. She is a frequent visitor to his home. I am very tired of his advances and decide to throw caution to the wind. Damn the consequences.

I walk away from him. I will spend the night on the couch. Patiently I wait until everyone leaves the home. Calmly, I make myself comfortable on the living room couch. When he realizes that I am not in his bed, he comes looking for me. Finding me on the couch, he tries persuading me to come to bed. But I'm adamant. After much talking, he comes to the realization that I'm not going to budge. My mind has been made up, and if he gets physical with me, I will scream, bringing the guests out of their rooms to find out what's going on. Sensing my determination not to cooperate, he tells me how disappointed he is in me, huffing off to his bed.

I couldn't care less how disappointed he is in me. So are my mother and father, and I don't give a damn any more. I have had enough of the abuse, and have to take a stand at some point in my life. I realize that if I continue allowing him to take advantage of me, this cycle will never end. I have survived him for years, have survived my mother for years, have survived a pregnancy, and now have a child to live for. The victim that I have become needs to stop being afraid of the consequences, and put up boundaries in her life. This is the first one to go up. I may have to pay dearly for it, because I know how calculating and cruel he can be to those who dare to deny him his desires. But I don't care, he can't kill me, so let him do whatever he wishes.

The business in St. Thomas is completed and we return to Kingston. I'm dropped off at my home, and I am delighted to see my baby girl as she comes running, flying into my arms. The problems of the past five days melt away as I embraced her, never wanting to leave her again. It's the weekend, so I'm able to spend two days doting on her. Work on Monday resumes as usual, with no discussions, but there is never been any discussion about the rapes. It amazes me that no one ever speaks about anything that happens in that house. It's almost as if a code of silence has been placed upon everyone who enters the halls.

Two weeks later, I'm surprised that my monthly cycle fails to make an appearance. With fear in my heart, I wait to see what will happen as the weeks progressed. Maybe I'm just late. Four weeks later I'm still late, and much to my chagrin, I wake up with morning sickness.

"Oh God no, this can not be happening. I can't be pregnant, and for whom? I'm really going to die this time."

I am totally devastated. It has only been one year since the birth to my daughter. Her father and I have never been intimate with each other again. I'm not even friendly with another man, so there is no doubt who is the father of this baby. Trouble has just taken up permanent residence at my door.

When my third period is missed, I know without a doubt that the most dreaded thing has befallen me again. I have told no one about my situation. At the end of a workday, I lag behind waiting for the other workers to leave. I tell my godfather about my condition. Feigning innocence, he begin telling me that he hopes the young man will stand up to his responsibilities, taking better care of me this time. Looking him in the eye I tell him, "There is no young man, the baby is yours."

He vehemently denies that such a thing could be possible. I remind him of his assault on me in St. Thomas and tell him that was when it happened.

"I have been with no one else. You are the one who forced yourself on me in St. Thomas."

He continues denying paternity, but I quickly put a stop to his statement.

"I have no doubt about whom the father is, because I have been with no one else. I have not had sex with anyone since before the birth of my baby, so I know for sure that it's yours."

This must frighten him; he cannot allow it to come to light. I leave for home, fighting for calm as my mind races around and around, trying to figure how on earth this is going to play out. I can see my baby and myself on the streets, because I'm under no illusion that my mother will continue keeping me at home during another pregnancy, just one short year later.

A couple weeks pass and on a few occasions he asks if I still felt the same way about him being the "Father of the fetus."

As he chose to refer to the pregnancy, I tell him, "Yes, and there is nothing to change."

I'm getting very worried. In another month it will become evident that I am pregnant and all hell will break loose again. I lose weight from worry and sleeplessness.

At about midday on Friday of that week, he tells me that he has made an appointment for me, with his doctor, Dr. Gripe, who is one of his best friends and confidant. He tells me he wants a confirmation of the age of the fetus, "so he could determine if it really belongs to him."

That's fine with me. I need to see a doctor anyway. The chauffeur is instructed to take me to Dr. Gripe. He gives me a sealed envelope addressed to the doctor. Knowing of their friendship, I think nothing of the envelope. I tell the nurse who I am and that I need to see the doctor to personally deliver correspondence from the Hon. M. H. Nowington, Minister of Government. Dr Gripe soon appears to greet me, and I deliver the envelope to him. A nurse tells me to wait; I will be the last patient. "That's okay," I say, making myself comfortable. The chauffeur leaves me.

The other patients have been seen, and I'm the only one left in the waiting room. The good doctor himself comes out to greet me again. We know each other, having met on several occasions at social gatherings. He has even visited the home a few times, but I have never been one of his patients. He invites me into his office asking about the "Man on the hill." I assure him he is fine.

He then asks what he could do for me. I tell him of my suspicions of pregnancy. He ushers me into an examination room, instructs me to get undressed, and get on the examination table, he will be right back. I have been through a prenatal exam before so I know what to expect. I get on the table and wait.

When he returns I notice he is carrying unfamiliar equipment in a dish, but ask no questions. He places them on a tray, but I had no reason to wonder what they are for. He asks the familiar questions to verify pregnancy. I answer honestly. After the examination, he verifies that I am pregnant and he needs to do a blood test to determine the age and predict the due date. I know this to be true, so I nod in agreement. He leaves me with my legs in the stirrups, telling me not to get dressed yet. He wants to do another exam. Uncomfortable as it isf I remain in this embarrassing position.

With his back turned he prepares a needle for what I think is to draw some blood for the tests. Instead, I have no time to object as he turns around, quickly inserting the needle into my hip, giving me a shot.

"Why did you give me an injection?"

"To make you comfortable."

"Comfortable for what?" I ask. He offers no answer. I fight to form the question in my mind again, but can't quite get it together. I'm drifting off into semi-consciousness, somewhere between sleep and being awake, in a type of twilight zone.

I don't know for sure how long I remain in that state. I am vaguely aware of him working between my legs. I feel pressure but am unable to fathom what's happening. When I return to consciousness, I notice that I am alone in the room. My legs are out of the stirrups and I'm lying flat on my back. I must have fallen asleep, because I have absolutely no recollection of anything except the memory of him working between my legs. A few minutes pass while I'm quietly lying there trying to figure out why I'm asleep on a table in a doctor's examination room. Not long afterward, he enters the room, asking if I was in pain.

"No, why would I be in pain?"

"Because I performed an abortion on you."

"What?" I exclaimed. "I did not ask you to perform an abortion."

"Those were my instructions."

"Whose instructions? I simply asked for an exam to verify my pregnancy."

"Miss McLaren, I followed the instructions you gave to me yourself. Now if you feel okay, please get dressed. I need to go home."

With that, he leaves the room.

Pressing my hands to my stomach I try to feel the spot from which my child has been yanked out of me without my permission. Tears course down my face. This man had just killed my baby without even the decency of telling me what he was about to do. I have not been given the opportunity to make an important decision. Now everything has truly been taken away from me. The fact that the pregnancy would be the cause of great problems and distress did not give them the right to abort it without my knowledge or consent. I am shaking with all types of emotions.

Slowly I get dressed, not sure how I should feel after what just happened. He leaves a sanitary pad on the bed, telling me to use it, as there will be some bleeding. I take his advice. Dr. Gripe escorts me to

95

the door telling me to take care, then retreats into his office leaving me to find my own way home. I board a bus and get myself home. As soon as I get home I begin experiencing sharp cramps in my stomach. I cannot care for Jessica and ask my sisters to look after her for me. "What's the matter?" they ask. "I have cramps," I reply, getting into bed. It's impossible to rest with a one-year-old who has not seen her mother all day, so I play with her in bed for a while. Thankfully, it's Friday and the family always retires to bed early on Friday nights after worship, as there is no television watching, homework or any work done after sunset.

The house quiets down for the night. I ask my sisters to take Jessica upstairs with them because I really have bad cramps. They comply. bringing her back to me after she fell asleep. I'm in great pain. I take four Tylenols, but they have no effect on the pain. Sweat pours from my face as I hug my body far into the night. Pain rips through my body. Labor pains had not been this intense. I begin feeling as if I'm going to die. With the pain comes a perfusion of bleeding. Nothing could stem the flow. The sanitary pads fill up fast as I drag myself to and from the bathroom.

The pain is unbearable. I have to get help. I cannot die from bleeding in front of my baby who wakes up from my groaning. She calls, "Mummy," and I instantly know I have to get help from my parents upstairs or I'm going to bleed to death. I take Jessica out of bed, set her down on the floor and tell her to go upstairs and get Mama.

"Go get Mama" I tell her. "Tell Mama that Mummy wants her."

She walks off repeating her instructions, but she is only one year old, and is afraid of the dark. She goes to the stairs but returns to me in fear of climbing the dark stairs alone. I try sending her again but realize she is too young to carry out such a mission.

"Okay," I tell her, "Come with Mummy, we have to go get Mama."

With my daughter tagging along behind me, I drag myself up the stairs with my blood dripping down my legs. I crawl up the 16 stairs to my parent's bedroom. As I crawl up, I contemplate what to tell them. One part of me wants to confide in them, but another part warns me that I will be blamed for what had happened, so I could not tell them the truth. By the time I get to the top of the stairs I'm in so much pain I don't care who knows what, I just need help. I open my parent's door calling out to them, awakening them. They see me prostrate on the floor with Jessica standing next to me.

They spring off the bed asking, "What's the matter with you?" They notice my bleeding and my father exclaims, "Oh my God! What happened to you?"

I make no reply, just said I'm in pain. My father helps me to my feet, sitting me up on the foot of the bed. My mother gets towels, packing them between my legs, trying to control the blood flow. I feel a contraction rip through me, and to my utter embarrassment, a huge placenta, falls right through the legs of my underwear plopping on the floor for everyone to see. They are shocked. I am ashamed, but right now all that have to wait. I still need help.

My sisters hear the commotion and come to ask what's happening. They are promptly sent back to bed and told to close the door. They obey taking Jessica, with them. The pain subsides after the placenta is expelled but the bleeding continues. For the first time, my mother comes to my aid, showing concern for me. She cleans me up and keeps asking me what was wrong. By now I have decided not to confide in her. I know the information would only be used against me later. So I close my mouth feigning ignorance of what had caused this pain and sever bleeding,

"Is this the first time your period is coming back since you had Jessica?" mother inquires.

I quickly take hold of that explanation, telling her yes. She seems satisfied with that answer.

I want to confide in my Mother. I want to tell her what Uncle Nowington and Dr. Gripe had done to me. I want to tell her about my heartaches and my hurts, I want to tell her about my pain and my frustrations, I want to tell my mother how much I am hurting, but I must keep my mouth shut. She has never been my confidant. How can I start confiding in her now? He has not only gotten away with numerous rapes, now he had ordered the murder of a child and will get away with it. Maybe this is a good time to go to the police. But who will believe me? Certainly Dr. Gripe will not testify against him, and which police officer will dare to read him his rights and arrest him?

97

When I'm able to move, Daddy helps me downstairs to the bathroom, then back into bed. He makes me comfortable, telling me to call him if I need help during the night. The experience is horrifying. I spend the rest of the night in mental agony. Earlier that day, I had been violated in the most dreadful way, was left to find my own way home, had not even been given one painkiller, but had been sent home to deal with what follows an abortion.

I realize that my life means nothing to these people; I'm simply a pawn to be used, abused and thrown away when my usefulness is over. My godfather has no problems raping me, but as soon as the consequences of his action was about to be made public, he wields his power. Hate and loathing for this man well up in me. The idea that the doctors orders had been delivered to him by my own hands in that sealed envelope sickens me, and to make matters worse, I'm expected to return to work on Monday – expected to function as if nothing out of the ordinary has happened.

On Monday morning I refuse to go to work. The car comes to pick me up and I send back a message saying I'm sick. In fact, I am very sick: my temperature has soared to 105 degrees, I'm hemorrhaging and I'm weak and lethargic. For three days I remain in bed, drinking tears, hugging my baby for companionship. For two weeks I stay away from work. The thought of facing him is so unbearable that I decide to look for another job. I go for a few interviews but when the employers discover for whom I work and that I had to give notice to leave his employment, they offer excuses for not being able to hire me. They are afraid of the consequences when he finds out that they have hired away one of his employees. I have a child to provide for, so I swallow my loathing and return to work

Not one word is spoken between us about what had transpired. He briefly inquires if I'm feeling better and I say yes. Work resumes as normal. But I do not return to normal . I feel a void deep within me that nothing can fill. I always cry easily, but this tendency is amplified. At the sight of a baby, I get teary eyed, and any conversation pertaining to childbirth brings on a deep longing within me. As the months pass, I find myself constantly keeping track of where my pregnancy would be now, and at the end of nine months I descend into deep private mourning for the death of a child whose life had so brutally ended.

I need healing. I need to talk to someone. I'm listening to the radio and hear the revelations of three women who have had abortions. I have buried the abortion deeply. I think I have it under control, but now the emotions rise to the surface, bringing a new wave of hysteria. I call the radio station. I talk with the host revealing to her the shame I have been bearing. I bear my soul to her, telling her about the abortion and how responsible I feel for the baby's death. I'm devastated. Tears are blinding me. Talking helps my aching soul, but healing does not come that day. If anything it serves to intensify my sorrow.

Wiping my tears, I tell myself, "Come on Marcia, don't let them see you cry. You can do this girl, you have to, and you have Jessica to think about." My life is never the same again. Hours are spent each night crying. My dreams are tormented. I dream of trying to find my daughter, something deep within me tells me it was a girl. In my dream she cries for me. Always I recognized the cries as that of my child, coming from a distance. I'm running through open and closed doors, down long hallways, down the street, through buildings, always looking, calling out to her, telling her.

"I am coming, sweetheart! Hold on, I'm coming!"

Always running, but never getting to her. Her cries ringing in my ears, my arms longing to hold her, to put her to my breast and provide food and comfort, longing to put her on my shoulders and rock her to sleep. I want to look into her eyes, touch her cheeks with my fingers, kiss her forehead and change her dirty diapers. But I never find her. At times she seems to be close, I can sense her presence I can almost reach out and touch her. If only I could find her. Where is she? Why can't I find her? Looking around one more bend, peering into the face of children, calling out to her.

"I am coming baby. You'll be alright. Mommy is coming to get you."

I'm jolted out of restless sleep. With tears running down my face, I enfold myself in my own arms, rocking myself, finding comfort in my empty arms. I cry out to God for help.

"O God, help me. I am pathetic and in need of your forgiveness and love. One of the children you gave to me is dead. I did not personally kill her, but feel responsible for her death. I know the little angel is in heaven with you. May you comfort her, because I can't. Please care for her, and Lord, please forgive me for the part I played in snuffing out her life before she had an opportunity to take her first breaths. I am nobody, just a pitiful girl born into the worst family imaginable. You have no reason to hear me, or even help me, but for my child's sake, please have mercy upon her soul."

Shortly after this, one of my older sisters, Lynnette, decides to migrate to Canada to join the others. About one month before her departure from the island, she asks me if I would like to occupy her apartment and take care of her three children until she's able to file and take them to Canada. This is the best offer I have ever had. This will give me the opportunity to move out of my mother's house.

"Yes, I'll be happy to move into your apartment. When are you leaving?" All the arrangements are made, and she leaves for Canada. I move in with my daughter. Caring for the three children is a pleasure. They are good children and I love them. The eldest daughter, Deirdre, is more like a younger sister than a niece. Our mother tries talking Lynnette out of leaving the children in my care, telling her that I can hardly care for my own child and myself so they should be left in her care. But Lynnette refuses the offer. She knows how cruel our mother is.

For the first time, I experience freedom. I'm free of my mother's control and I have my own place. We settle in nicely, and my little household is happy. But happiness does not last long. In a couple weeks, my mother decides that regardless of what Lynnette wants, the children should have been left in her care. She does not want the children in her care because she loves them; it all comes down to money. She knows that as soon as Lynnette begins working, money will be sent back to Jamaica to care for the children, and the thought of her not receiving these funds are unbearable to her. She has to get these children in her home.

One fine evening, we are all at home enjoying a quiet end to a busy day and like a bad penny, here comes Mother. She orders the children to pack their stuff and get themselves to her home. They refuse. I refuse to let them go, reminding her that if their mother wanted them to be with her she would have left them with her. Nothing we say fazes her. She actually produces a belt and begins beating the children into obedience. Short of physically fighting her there is little I can do. Caring for my nieces and nephew comes to an end. Lynnette is furious when I call and tell her what happened, but no amount of talking will make mother send them back. They now live with their grandmother, but at least I still have my freedom.

Jessica and I are doing fine on our own. I continue working for my godfather, and even continue leaving her in her grandmother's care during the days, but with delight, I pick up my baby and retreat to my own apartment at the end of each day. I am happy. Finally, my life seems as if I am getting a handle on it. Making my own decisions, paying my rent, doing our laundry it's a little piece of heaven on earth. My sisters visit often, and they too enjoy the freedom from Mother's constantly watchful eyes. The biggest thrill of all is when there is a disagreement between her and Daddy, and she leaves him no dinner, he no longer has to purchase something from the store. He simply comes to visit me and I gladly feed him. He comes by often, just to get a little peace. When she discovers his whereabouts, she fumes. But we have learnt to ignore her.

Henry visits us regularly also. He has gotten a divorce and begins asking me to marry him. But as often as he asks, I refuse the offer. Too many unpleasant things have occurred, too many hurts, too many broken promises. I have survived the pregnancy without him at my side, and now feel that I want to find my own way without him. He is a link to the past and I want a fresh start. I prefer to meet someone new, someone who I will not associate with the pain of the last few years. Maybe then I can find healing and some peace. I'm also a little afraid of how the tongues of the church members will wag, and cannot see myself being happy among them. Maybe if I voice my concerns he will make the necessary changes to make me comfortable and happy. But I had been so scared, that I just want a new beginning with new people. The future of my child and myself depends upon me being able to establish some sort of stability to our lives. As long as I continue working for the enemy I will continue to be violated. But hope has returned, it burns deep within my heart.

One day we will overcome.

Chapter Ten

LOSS OF ANOTHER CHILD

few months later, I meet a handsome young man. As I walk pass a bar, someone whistles. I look around with a smile on my face, and there, lounging by the door with a glass of dark liquid in one hand and a cigarette in the other, is Chad. I like what I see, so I walk back to speak with him. We introduce ourselves, talk for a few minutes, then exchange telephone numbers. I do not have a telephone at home, but as soon as I arrive at work on Monday morning, he is on the line asking to speak with me. He likes to party, and invites me to accompany him to one on Saturday night. Before long we become a couple.

Each weekend we go out on dates to nightclubs and bars. I'm being introduced to partying and nightlife. I discover that I have an affinity for this life – the music, the dancing, the smell of liquor mixed with cigarette smoke, the tantalizing lights, and the rhythm of the music. It excites me to no end. We have a great deal of fun, especially during the weekends. I frequently leave Jessica with my sisters while I go off partying with my new friend.

He is introduced to my parents and sisters. Daddy and my sisters like him, and surprisingly enough, Mama approves of him. She likes his light colored skin and his head of beautiful black curly hair. He is not a member of her faith, but neither am I. At this point, I simply want to enjoy my life. Religion has no place in it. Six months into our relationship I become pregnant. This time I'm not devastated. I'm 20 years old and mature. I have my own place and am living my own life. Having another baby is not what I need, but the inevitable has happened and I cannot change it.

My mother notices the change in my stomach and asks if I'm pregnant. I tell her it's none of their business. Chad partially moves in with me, but he has the tendency to return to his mother's home, with whom he still lives whenever we have a disagreement, sleeping there two to three nights per week. I have no idea which night he'll be with me or when he chooses to go home to Mama. He's 28 years old. This irritates me to no end, but I'm learning to deal with it.

The day I decide to tell him that I'm pregnant, I call him at work, verifying that he will be at my apartment that night. I plan a special romantic evening: preparing his favorite meal, accompanied by candlelight and music. Jessica is sent to spend the night with my sisters.

Everything works according to plan. We enjoy a nice meal, listen to music, dance together. Then, retiring to bed, I say, "I have something to tell you."

"Go ahead, I'm listening."

"I'm pregnant."

I'm a little apprehensive about what his reaction will be, but he quickly assures me that he is happy about the pregnancy and will be supportive. I'm relieved, but relief quickly turns to anger when he says that he also has something to tell me. My heart leaps. What is it? Is he married and had been keeping it a secret?

Earlier in our relationship he told me that he had fathered a child when he was 18 years old, and that his daughter lives with her mother in another part of the city.

"What do you have to tell me?" I ask.

"You are not going to like hearing this, but I have another child: a son, his name is Gregory. He is six years old and lives with his mother in Sunrise. I see him often, but his mother is now married and there is nothing between us."

This news hits me like a ton of bricks. It's better than if he had been married, but I'm still angry that he had kept this from me.

Angrily I ask. "Is there anything else I need to know about you while we're making confessions?"

"No Marcia, I have no secrets. There are no more skeletons in the closet."

"I don't want to be lied to. I'll be very upset if, down the road, I find out that you have been keeping things from me."

"I promise you, my dear, that there is nothing more in my life that I need to reveal to you. I love you and will be looking forward to the birth of our baby."

"I love you, too."

Lying there in the dark listening to his steady breathing I reflect on the thought that he is the father of two children. I'm still mad that he had not told me before, but I have no right to be mad. After all, I have not breathed one word of my sordid past to him. Except for the fact that I have a child, he knows nothing about me. The idea to tell him about my past crosses my mind, but the thought is quickly squashed, remaining locked away in the secret files of my mind.

There are no upheavals in my life. Things remain on an even kneel. We settle into a routine. By this time, Bridget and Janice are in separate colleges, both pursing teaching careers. Bridget commutes to school, but Janice lives on campus. Cheryl, Anton, my nieces and my nephew are the only children in the home now. They are still ruled by an iron hand, but Mother doesn't dare sell Lynnette's daughters in the fashion she had sold her own.

I speak to her only about the care of my child. She is not encouraged to visit me at my home. So one Sunday morning when she shows up uninvited and unannounced at my home, she gets what she deserves. Ignoring me, she marches through my front door and into my bedroom. Chad is asleep in bed, and she is shocked to see a man in my bed. She rushes out of the room while I stand there with a smirk on my face.

"Why didn't you tell me there was a man in your room?" she questioned

"You did not ask. You simply walked into my bedroom without permission. What do you want?"

"To see my grandchild"

"As you can see she's asleep. Now I'm a big woman turning my own key in my own door. The next time you wish to make a visit to my home, please let me know first."

"Don't worry I'll never set foot in this door again. This is exactly why I took Lynette's children from you – because I don't know what kind of slackness you are carrying on around here."

"You have no reason to check up on Jessica; you'll see her tomorrow. You just wanted to pry into my business. Goodbye Mama."

In a huff, she turns on her heels and walks away, never returning to my humble abode.

In my eight month of pregnancy, I ask Chad to reposition the furniture in the bedroom to make room for a bassinet for the new baby. He says he'll get around to it. I ask twice, getting the same answer. "I'll get around to it."

It's Christmas time and I want it done now. But he has not gotten around to it yet. The New Year roars in and he still has not gotten around to it. So I decide to do it myself. In his absence, I take on the task of moving Jessica's crib. I move the dresser and the other furniture around. While pushing and tugging the dresser, I feel a sharp pain in my back. Stopping what I'm doing, I sit down on the bed. In a few minutes another pain – this time of greater magnitude – assails my body. I'm in trouble. The neighbors with cars have left for work, and there is no telephone in the apartment.

My neighbor, Stacy, and her mother share an apartment next door. She also has a little girl who is Jessica's playmate. Thankfully they are home. Hobbling outside, I knock on their door, Stacy opens it, and I tell her what's happening. I need to get to the hospital quickly. Stacy runs to the street, hails a taxi, and jumps into the car, accompanying me to my mother's home where I know that Bridget is still on Christmas vacation from school. Telling her what's going on, she yells the news to Mama, then gets into the taxi with me.

The ride to the hospital seems to be taking forever. It becomes evident that the baby was not going to wait. My sister begs the driver to drive faster. He tries, but morning traffic on Kingston Street is a nightmare. He tells me to hold on, but matters are out of my control. I cry out in pain, feeling the uncontrollable urge to push and knowing what it means.

"The baby is coming," I warn.

"Try to hold on," I'm encouraged.

I try holding on, I try very hard not to push by squeezing my pelvic muscles together as tight as I can, but to no avail. In the back seat of the taxi, with the driver frantic and without medical help, my baby is born. We don't know what to do. I knew that my water had not broken, but did not know the significance of that. My baby is born in a sac, but none of us know what to do. We yell to the driver to hurry. Shortly after the birth we arrive at the hospital and the driver flies out of the car running to get help. They come running with a wheelchair. The nurse sizes up the situation rushing us into the emergency room yelling for a doctor to come at once.

Immediately a medical team surrounds us. They cut the umbilical cord, rushing off with the baby. While the nurse is taking care of me, I ask about the baby.

"How is my baby doing? We didn't know what to do, should we have broken the sac that he was in?"

"The doctors are working on him. We'll let you know his condition soon."

"Him? Do I have a son?"

"Yes it's a boy. The doctor will talk to you as soon as he can."

I wait for the nurse to bring my son to me, just the way it had happened last time. But instead, after about 30 minutes, the doctor comes into my room, grim faced. I know something is wrong. I look from one face to the other as the doctor begins speaking.

"We did our best to save your baby, but he spent too much time in the sac, he drowned in the fluid, and to make matters worse, the umbilical cord was wrapped around his neck cutting off oxygen from his brain. Even if he had survived he would probably have suffered severe brain injury or been a vegetable. I'm sorry."

I cannot believe what I'm hearing. My baby is dead. Everything within me moves in agony, and I begin retching, spewing vomit all over the bed. It was such a violent reaction that it takes the doctor by surprised. I scream and cry, and they clean me up, changing the bed linen. The harsh reality is, I have lost my baby, and it is entirely my fault. The doctor asks if I would like to see him, and I tell him no. I know that I would not survive looking at his lifeless body, so I refuse to take a glimpse of my son.

After some time, Bridget is allowed to visit me. She cries with me trying to console me. She had gotten a glimpse of him, and tells me how beautiful he was, with a full head of black hair. But no amount of crying can bring him back to life; he is gone forever. Chad still has no idea that his baby has died. He had left for work, and no one has thought of calling him. There had been no time to make the call.

Visiting hours are over and Bridget leaves. I think it's a cruel thing to place a mother who has lost her baby in the same room with other mothers of live babies. As I listen to the mothers quietly talking to their babies, encouraging them to suck, comforting those who cry and hearing the happiness in their voices, I fall apart. I wail so loudly that the nurse, before giving me a sedative ordered by the doctor, tells me that if I cry like this I will make myself sick. She also tells me that the only way to recover from the lost of a baby is to have another one as soon as possible. I don't want to hear anything about another child. I want my son. But no miracles could be performed. He is gone and I have to go on.

The next day after, the doctors visit their patients. I'm told that although I had experienced such an awful loss, I have been released. The doctor offers, "You are young and healthy and need healing of the spirit which we cannot provide. Go home and take care of yourself. Sometimes things happen for the best, even though they don't seem that way at first." I feel like smacking him in his face. Instead, I turn my face to the wall to hide my tears.

Again, there is no one waiting to take me home. I don't even know if my sisters had been able to contact Chad to tell him what has happened. I'm wheeled out the front door, and just like two years earlier, the porter gets me a taxi to take me home. The difference this time is that I return empty-handed. Returning to the empty apartment is more than I can bear. A feeling of complete desolation sweeps over me. Throwing my head back, I emit a scream like none before. It fills the apartment, bringing my neighbors running.

I am standing in the doorway, empty-handed, so they figure out what has happened and came to my aid. They hug and cry with me. Stacy helps me into bed, and stays for a while. Later that evening, Chad comes home. For the first time, he learns that his son has died. He sits down hard on the bed, covers his face with his hand and weeps.

108

"Why didn't someone tell me what happened? Why wasn't I called? You were in the hospital. The baby died two days ago and no one called me. Why?"

"It all happened so fast there was no time to call you. You know there are no telephones in the hospital rooms, and I was just released this morning. If you had come home last night, you would have found out."

"O my God, this is awful. I should have been there for you. I'm sorry you had to go through this alone. I promise to at least stop by every evening on my way home from work. I'm sorry I wasn't here. Please forgive me," he begs. "O my God, this is terrible. Are you all right?"

"No I am not alright," I reply. "My baby just died. I feel like dying myself because I feel responsible for his death. I don't know how I'm going to survive this. O God, help me."

In each other's arms we cry for what seems like an eternity. There we draw comfort from each other. We will have to get through this.

My sisters bring Jessica home, and I hold her tightly, pouring all my love into her.

Four weeks later, I return to work and everyone wants to know what happened. I tell the story once and tell them not to ask about it again, because it's too difficult of an experience to be related again. Taking pity on me, they put the subject to rest, at least in my presence. Over time, I return to normal. I pretend to be all right but I'm not. The reel of the events never stops playing in my mind. It doesn't matter what activity I'm engaged in, there is no stopping it. I cannot forgive myself, and cry constantly for what I have done. If only I had not been so impatient. If only I had waited. If only...

If I thought I was being tormented before, my own private hell has only just begun. Now instead of dreaming of one lost child, I have two precious little souls looking for their mother. Don't ask me how, but in my dreams, my dead children have found each other. Hand in hand, two pairs of little feet patter around looking for their mom. Two distinct voices, two babies crying for mommy. I am roaming through bushes, corridors, and rooms. Looking into cribs, under beds; under tables; in closets; into the faces of every child I pass, knowing I'll recognized mine. Looking everywhere for my children.

"Mommy! Mommy!" Both voices call out to me in unison. "Where are you my babies?" I call out to them. "I'm trying to find you! I'm coming. I'll be right there."

My son was born and died on January 6, 1978. Two children have now been lost. I can either live in my grief or recover and live for the one I have. I decide that I will never forget my other two children, but the one who is alive needs me. I manage to get on with my life, but always secretly mourn my losses, always crying for the children I have never held in my arms.

No one shares in my private torment – I speak of it to no one.

Chapter Eleven

TWO NEW BABIES

At my parents home one evening, there is an abnormal, expectant hush in the air. Cheryl, our youngest sister, seems petrified with a wild look in her eyes.

"What's going on?" I ask.

She escorts me outside, and in a hushed voice she tells me that she is pregnant, and that the father of the baby is coming over to tell our parents.

"What, O my God, Mama is going to kill you."

I am flabbergasted with the unexpected news. She is only 15, two years younger than I was when I got pregnant, and is a high school senior. I'm genuinely sorry for her.

"But it gets worst," she continues, "The father is one of my teachers from school."

O Lord, what is this? Now we're going to have two dead people. I'm going no place. This, I have to see and hear. I linger talking with her, telling her that she can come and live with me if she wants to. That cheers her up a bit, but not for long, as there is a knock at the gate. The brave young man has arrived. I quickly ask him if it's true and he confirms it. He also assures me that he is more than capable and willing to take full responsibility for his actions. He has no idea of what he is up against.

I ask how and when this happened and he tells me how on several occasions he invited Cheryl to his home, using the pretense of

111

helping her with her homework. He had taken a great liking to her, and admits to taking advantage of her vulnerability. He is aware of the possibility of great trouble for him, being an adult in a position of authority becomng sexually involved with a minor. He is trying to be brave, and is doing what he thinks to be the right thing.

Trouble looms large. Mother arrives home and asks why there is a strange man in her home. None of us answers. He introduces himself, plunging right in with both feet. Without missing a beat, he tells her exactly who he is and why he's there. Anger is not an adequate description of her reaction. She vows to make him pay in more ways than he can even imagine for what he has done, then she kicks him out of the house. Then she turns on Cheryl.

"Another disgrace, another disappointment, another reason to hang my head in shame. None of you are any good. I sent you to school to learn how to spell your name so you wouldn't eat it on a bulla, not to sleep with your teacher. What the hell is wrong with the lot of you? Aren't any of you going to come out to be any good? I have only wasted my time and effort on all of you. I wish I had killed all of you at birth. Oh my God, I can't take any more of this. I can't go through this again. Find somewhere else to live and get out of my house. Get out of my sight."

I again offer my sister my home as a place of refuge, but mother overhears the conversation and refuses to allow her to leave the house. She doesn't want her there, but will not let her leave, either. Within a few months, her life becomes unbearable with the constant abuse. She tells the father of her baby about her home situation. He comes by with his car, moving her out of the home placing her in his mother's home. We visit her there. She continues attending school until graduation.

Our dear mother has to have her revenge. She reports the young man's conduct to the School Board, and following an investigation into the charges he loses his job. He finds employment elsewhere but there is no hiding from her fury. Mother discovers where he works, and reports him to his employers as a child molester and rapist, which ultimately leads to his dismissal.

On my visit to the doctor for my postnatal exam, I make a request for and am given oral contraception. The thought of getting pregnant again is not appealing. Being healthy and having never taken regular medication, I have a hard time remembering to take the pills. Sometimes I miss days then I take two or more pills, trying to make up for the missed doses. I don't know what I'm doing. I only know that I don't want to get pregnant again.

Peggy is an older woman who gives free and sometimes unwanted advice to the younger woman in the apartment complex. She often relates stories about her life and some of her struggles, raising her children without the help of her husband who left the family to form another family, forgetting about her and his six children. She has what we called in Jamaica a "goat's mouth." Meaning, whatever she says almost always come to pass.

About two months after I lost my son, she looks at me with those narrowed piercing eyes, uttering deafening words: "You are going to get pregnant very soon again."

"Not over my dead body."

"Whether you body is dead or alive, you are going to get pregnant soon. Your body is ripe for a baby."

"What does that mean?" I ask her

"When a woman loses a baby, no matter what she does, as long as she has a man in her bed, she gets pregnant soon afterwards."

"I am taking the pill, so that won't be true in my case."

"You can take all the pill you want. As long as that man you have in there is sleeping with you, another baby will be on the way soon."

Laughing at her, I dismiss her prediction as another of her old wives' tales. I share her prediction with Chad.

"Whatever will be will be," he sums it up. "No one knows the future. If it happens we'll deal with it."

We certainly do not know the future, and Peggy does have a goat's mouth. Because two months later I discover that I'm pregnant again. I'm not excited. I think it's too soon after the loss, and I am concerned about my body's ability to properly sustain another baby so soon. I had given birth to my son in January, and this is only April – too soon to go through another pregnancy. But regardless of what I think, another baby had been conceived, and its life has to be sustained.

Chad's family and I have grown close. His mother is a lovely lady, and his brothers and sisters are great people. Three of the adult's sons still live at home, including Chad, who still sleeps there whenever he feels like it. I tell their mother she has spoiled them. She agrees, but does not encourage them to leave and fend for themselves. With this second pregnancy, Chad and I begin talking about getting married. I want to, and would love to be his wife, but I'm having concerns about him being so tied to his mother's apron string. I decide to talk to his mother about my concerns. Visiting her on a Sunday afternoon, over cool drinks I tell her about the new pregnancy and about the step we are thinking about taking. She smiles at me, tells me how much she likes me, that she think I am a wonderful young lady who would make a good wife, but that I should not waste my time marrying Chad.

"I am pregnant again and he says he is tired of living like a bachelor. He agrees that we should provide a stable home for the children."

"My dear, Chad is just like his father who left me with nine children to care for on my own. Of all the boys, he is most like his father. See how often he leaves you alone and comes here at nights? That's exactly what he'll do, even when you are married. He doesn't like responsibilities, and I'm sorry to tell you, but if you marry him, he won't change. His father was the same way, until one day he left and never came back. I suggest you have the baby. He'll support both of you, but if you try to tie him down with marriage, he'll run."

I'm crushed, but something inside of me tells me that what she says is the harsh truth. He always leaves our place at the slightest hint of a disagreement, staying away for days before returning. But I keep thinking that he will change his ways once we become husband and wife. His mother has dashed these hopes, and for once in my life, I decide to heed the advice of someone who knows what she's talking about. I can't help being pregnant, but I can stop myself from being stuck in an unhappy marriage. I know what it feels like to be in an unhappy home. If at any time he wants his freedom, I will not stand in his way.

That night I tell Chad that we need more time to get to know each other better. If after the baby's birth he still feels the same way, we will get married then. With almost a sigh or relief he agrees. I'm thankful to his mother for giving me an honest answer regarding her son. He is fun to be with, but he does not portray the ability to provide the stability that I'm looking for and need. When the party is over and reality stares us in the face, he does not seem to have the gumption to square his shoulders and take on whatever life brings his way. Instead he retreats to Mama's house and goes to sleep. We have a baby to prepare for, and right now my most important task is to take care of myself, and protect both of my children, born and unborn.

Chad is not as good a provider as I hoped he would be. He makes a good salary, but continues partying and hanging out with his friends at nights, spending too much money on the street instead of in his home. I'm pretty much responsible for making all the preparations for the baby. I find myself calling him at work, telling him that I need his financial help to prepare for the baby. He hates confrontations, making it almost impossible for us to have serious conversations or make long-term plans. Jessica and I spend many Sunday afternoons at his mother's home. She welcomes us, whether he is there or not. I became attached to her, finding in her what my own mother has never given to me.

During one of our frequent conversations about the sex of the baby, Chad expresses his desire for a son. I want another daughter. I can envision an angelic face with masses of black curly hair, just like her dad's. I dream of how beautiful a child between us will be, and cannot envision having to cut off those beautiful curls instead of allowing them to hang down the little girl's back. I talk to her, sing to her, assuring her that regardless of what happens it will be my babies and me against the world.

My pregnancy so soon after my loss surprises everyone. My godfather comments on it and I simply ignore his comments. I stay away from my parent's home, instead asking my sisters to bring Jessica home in the evenings for me. My mother's opinion of the obvious is of no interest to me. The path my life is heading down is not ideal, but I'm struggling to come to terms with everything that has happened, desperately trying to find myself.

I'm 21 years old and pregnant for the fourth time. My first child is three years old, the second one had been aborted without my consent, and the third one died. The fourth will be born in the same year. This may seem like promiscuous behavior to most people, but I'm not living an irresponsible life style. Unfortunate events have happened and the pregnancies are the result of some of these events. The enormity of the situation is not lost on me, but now that I am more mature and have the life long responsibility of caring for these innocent children, definite changes will be made in my life. After the birth of this baby, the use of a more-reliable contraceptive will be practiced. If Chad and I do not get married, I will not bring another child into the world under these circumstances.

Cheryl is almost at her due date. Mother wants her home so she can have more control over her life – beating her into the ground, breaking her spirit. Her baby's father refuses to bring her back. That does not deter mother. She makes such a stink at his mother's home that Cheryl is encouraged to pack her bags and leave with her mother. On September 4, 1976, Cheryl gives birth to a beautiful baby girl. The father is present at the hospital for his daughter's birth. Mother makes his life miserable, but he sticks to his word and does not abandon his child. The beautiful baby girl is named Nadine Denise Roseanne. She is beautiful, as precious as the most priceless jewels of the queen of Sheba. We all love her.

December arrives, and I'm in the eight month of my pregnancy. I decide to continue working until the end of the year. Friday the 29th will be my last day in the office. At the end of an exhausting day I go home, planning to return on Saturday to clean off my desk, put files in order, and be off on three months maternity leave. My baby's due date is early January of next year.

On my doctor's advice, we made arrangements for a midwife who lives nearby to deliver my baby at home. He's concerned that I may have a repeat of the last episode, because of the distance from the hospital. We have had a few meetings with this lovely lady. She gave us instructions of how to prepare for the birth as soon as I'm in labor. I share her instructions with my sisters, whom I hope will be around to provide the support I need.

Very tired after a long day at work. I lay down to rest, and shortly after I'm forced out of bed by hunger pangs. Cooking is not on the agenda. So Sharon and I walk over to a restaurant to purchase a bowl of soup. Back in my apartment Sharon brings me a slice of hot potato

116

pudding, straight from the oven. It is washed down by a bottle of cold cream soda…Mmm, delicious!

Almost immediately there is a burning in my stomach. I figure it's heartburn from eating that piece of pudding too fast. Two antacids go down the hatch. The heartburn persists, and I go to bed. My sisters and my niece brings Jessica home, finding me reclining in bed. "What wrong?" they ask.

"I have such a bad heartburn," I tell them.

"What did you eat?" They have often chided me about my poor diet.

"Just a bowl of soup, a slice of potato pudding, and a bottle of soda, " I reply.

"And you wonder why you have heartburn?..."

Without warning, a contraction rips through my body. I gasp for air, grabbing my stomach. A second contraction follows with more intensity. I am in labor. My sister and niece hurry to get Miss Price, the midwife, while between contractions I tell Bridget and Alicia to boil a pot of water, gather several towels and plastic bags. Taking a shower means hanging on to the walls as contractions rip through my body. I hope Chad comes home soon.

The contractions are coming so quickly together that I begin to fear the baby will get here before Miss Price does. She gets here not a minute too soon. She assesses the situation, puts on her gloves and gown, giving quick instructions to my sisters. Behind the closed bedroom door, with six pairs of twitching ears glued to the door they listen to hear me scream. I bite my lips until it bleeds, grinding my teeth together. I push hard and do what I have to do. But not one scream escapes my throat.

After only four hours of labor, at 11:45 pm, Friday December 29, 1978, my second daughter enters the world, clearing her lungs with her first cry. Miss Price changes the sheets, gathering the used items. She makes me comfortable and places my daughter in my arms.

An angel. That's the only way to describe her. A perfect little angel has descended from heaven, blessing me with her presence. All six and one-quarter pounds, twenty inches of her are every mother's dream. Her perfectly formed head, and her sweet face glows with life. Her full head of black hair is like running your fingers through silken threads. Her features are as if formed by the very hands of God himself, as He lovingly shaped her forehead, straightened her nostrils, kissed her lips and set her jaw at just the right angle. Her fingers lovingly curl around my finger as I kiss each one. She is gorgeous, and I love the beautiful sight, savoring the delicious smell of her, holding her close to my heart.

Miss Price completes her work and opens the door. My sisters are all standing there, waiting for news of us. The room has been quiet, except for the sound of a crying newborn infant. They come in full of excitement. "How come we didn't hear anything? We thought you would be screaming. Didn't it hurt? O my goodness, look at her. She is beautiful."

She is gorgeous. In hushed voices they exclaim at her beauty. Very carefully she is placed in the arms of her big sister Jessica, who thinks she has just been given a new doll.

Nicole Amanda, nicknamed Nia. She takes a firm hold on the hearts of her family. Her Daddy has no idea that his daughter has been born. We still have no telephone. He will just have to wait until he shows up to partake in her essence. Placing her on my chest, I begin singing to her. I know I'm off key, but she doesn't care. One of my sisters spends the night with us. I drift off into sleep.

Saturday morning dawns bright and beautiful. As the neighbors awake and news of the late arrival is made known, other neighbors visit to wish us well, each bringing a covered dish. They stop by to catch a glimpse of the little one. I proudly show her off even as she peacefully sleeps.

Chad shows up Saturday afternoon, almost falling over when he realizes what had happened. He is disappointed that he missed her birth. I try hard not to say it serves you right. He is in awe of her, holding her for hours; even while she sleeps.

After the first seven days of her life, I begin noticing that when she is touched, there is yellow tint left on her. Her eyes are not as clear as they should be. I'm concerned, but the midwife will be visiting in two days. So I wait.

Miss Price shows up for a visit she make sure I am doing well. I explain my concern about the yellowing of Nia's skin. She tells me that the blood, which had been drawn at birth, had been tested and the results revealed that my baby is seriously jaundiced. "What does this mean? Is she going to be all right?"

Miss Price gently tells me that if Nia had been born in the hospital she would have been placed under an ultraviolet lamp for hours to decrease the bilirubin in her blood. She now needs to be placed under this light daily to avoid liver damage. How can I do this? I do not drive and I'm not sure if Chad will be able to take the time necessary. The only other alternative is for me to sit in the morning sun holding her for about four hours each morning. I have to be careful to protect her eyes from the direct sunlight.

For one month I sit outside with my baby across my lap, exposing one section of her for a few minutes, turning her over at intervals to prevent burning her skin. Slowly her skin tone improves, and her yellowed eyes become clear. Through all this discomfort she was still a very happy child, crying rarely.

Another problem raises its ugly head. Her belly button protrudes, forming into a large knot, growing right along with her. The doctors examine the protrusion, shaking their heads, commenting that they have never seen such a large umbilical hernia. One specialist suggests surgery, but is quick to tell me that one has never been performed on a child under the age of five years old. But he is concerned with the rapid growth of Nia's stomach distension. He explains that the cavity in the navel is a serious problem. Her intestines have the potential to become entangled, causing an even greater problem. Nia has been experiencing trouble with digestion, a direct result of the umbilical hernia.

At the time of Nia's birth, Cheryl's daughter, Nadine, is three months old. She has a difficult time attaching herself to her mother's breast and refuses to take the bottle. We are concerned about her nutrition and I suggest trying to feed her. On the very first attempt, she grasps my breast with her lips, hanging on for dear life. She sucks until she is full. From that day, and for the next six months, I become her mother. I breastfeed both babies as if they were twins, sometimes feeding them at the same time. All three children are growing up as sisters.

At six weeks, Nia and I make a scheduled visit to the pediatrician's and my OB/GYN's office. Nia's blood test reveals that her jaundice is under control, but her stomach cavity is weak. Her umbilical hernia has been getting progressively worst. Surgery will be necessary as soon as she is old enough. During the visit to my gynecologist, I adamantly tell him that I want a permanent form of contraception. Tubal Ligation, he tells me is the most effective contractive, with a 99% success rate. When can I have it done? He refuses to perform the procedure, citing that I am young and unmarried, therefore I do not make a good patient for such a permanent procedure. Instead he educates me on the reliability of the intrauterine device (IUD), and I gladly agree and have the device inserted into my uterus.

Nia's recovery from jaundice does not last. She needs more than sunlight. In a couple months, her skin turns bright yellow and she becomes very ill. We take her to the hospital where she is admitted. The ultraviolet treatment is not as successful as hoped. The doctor decides that she needs a blood transfusion to save her from permanent liver damage. Her father's blood is tested and found to be suitable. We spend tense hours in the hospital waiting room until we are finally able to hold our baby in our arms again. We hope that she is going to be all right.

Before receiving the transfusion, Nia's illness is constant. We are always at the doctor's office or hospital emergency room for one ailment or another. She is truly a beautiful child, a pleasure to have around. Through all her illnesses, her personality remains cheerful, which prompts another observation from my neighbor, Peggy. We had just come in from sitting out in the sun one morning when Peggy takes a look at us, remarking, "That child is not going to live. She is too pretty. Those pretty babies usually don't live"

I am furious. How could she say such a thing to me after she had so recently witnessed the loss of my son? Fuming I face her.

"She is going to live; if I have to give my life for her, she is going to live. Whatever I have to do, she will live. You're an awful person for saying such a thing about a baby," I berate Peggy. "She will live. You'll see." I hug my baby tightly to my chest and cry at the pronouncement that has been made on her life and I pray, "Please God take care of my baby, please make her live."

She lives. Thank God, but her young life is full of constant illnesses, and surgeries. She recovers from her jaundice, but another problem arises. We notice the constant pulling on her ear lobe, and when her temperature spikes to 104 degrees, we rush her to the doctor's office. She has an inner ear infection. This becomes chronic and tubes are inserted into her ears.

It is amazing how one child can be so healthy and the other so plagued with illnesses. The appearance of large tumors on her buttocks surprise us, and and off to the hospital we go again. The doctors diagnose an allergic reaction to Milo. They keep appearing all over her body, necessitating many trips to the hospital to have them surgically removed. Each tumor leaves an indentation on her body. She will have many reminders of her childhood illnesses.

Watching Nia crawl is pitiful. Her distended hernia is of such magnitude that she appears to have three legs. This huge growth drags along behind her on the floor as she makes her way around the apartment. When she stands erect, the hernia looks like an elephant's trunk, and it also distorts her little body. It's difficult to securely fasten her diapers and her clothes do not fit properly. She is under the constant supervision of specialists who shake their heads, as they discuss the rapid growth of her hernia.

Nia turns 15 months old, and her doctors call us in for a conference with a specialist. They are very concerned with the growth of the hernia. They tell us that although they have never performed this surgery on a child under the age of five years, our baby's condition warrants it. They are worried that her intestines are becoming entangled, causing more problems.

We know she has digestive problems. The medical team proposes performing the surgery in three months, when she will be a year-and-a-half. With great apprehension, we discuss this turn of events, agreeing to allow the surgery. We take our baby home, fussing over her, showering her with love. We wish she could be spared until she is older, but her condition needs to be rectified now.

On the morning of the surgery, we awake to torrential rain as though the angels are weeping for this little one who is about to endure her ordeal. Chad and I bundle her up, and off we go to the hospital. The nurses prepare her for surgery. An intravenous needle is placed in her little arm. They draw her blood and record her vitals.

We had been instructed to withhold food from the previous evening so she is hungry, but we cannot feed her.

The doctor speaks with us, and then our baby is wheeled away to surgery. I am almost paralyzed with fear. The surgeon told us that general anesthetic would be administered to her. The rain suits our mood. Today is the hardest Chad and I have experienced as parents. Hours pass with us knowing nothing about her condition. We notice that all the other parents who were waiting for children in surgery have been called to their children's side – except for us, gloomily sitting there holding hands, waiting for words about our precious Nia.

A lifetime later a nurse approaches and asks us to follow her. We are led to the recovery room, there we're told that our baby has experienced an adverse reaction to the anesthetic, and they are having problems reviving her. The nurse instructs me to try to wake her up. My heart is heavy with fear. What has happened to her? She appears to be in a deep sleep. Reaching down into the bed I pat her back, together we stroke her head, brushing her cheeks. We call her name; I pick her up holding her in my arms, rocking and calling her name. But she sleeps on.

She is breathing ever so softly; the nurse brings us a chair. I sit down rocking and bouncing my baby on my knees. We take turns doing as much as possible to make her open her eyes. An hour later her eyes flutter.

With glazed pupils, she looks around trying to catch a glimpse of something or someone familiar. Our hearts soar with joy. She is alive, we hold her close to our bosoms, kissing her. Her vitals are checked, and I'm given a small amount of glucose to feed her. She is hungry crying for more. Crying could loosen the stitches in her abdomen. That's one of the reasons this surgery is usually not done prior to age five. Babies cry.

She needs to remain in the hospital overnight, and her release depends on how well she recovers She is transferred to a room and I have every intention of spending the night by her side, but the nurses insist that we leave. I beg them to allow me to spend the night with her, but they refuse. Reluctantly we kiss her, leaving her in the cold hospital room.

Two days later, we take her home with special instructions. She should not be allowed to cry. The incision needs to heal and crying will prolong the process. The area has to be cleaned and dressed daily. My queasy stomach barely allows me to perform this task, but it needs to be done. For the next two weeks, we watch her with eagle's eyes. Our weekly doctor's visits confirm that she is making good progress.

At work, my godfather tells me to go and have passport pictures taken – I will be needing a passport and a Visa to travel to Miami with him. I get my pictures taken, fill out the passport form, and the documents are placed into an envelope and sent down to the passport office with the chauffer. One week later, another sealed package is delivered by courier, addressed to me. Inside is my passport with a ten-year American Visa. Awesome! I have an American Visa! What am I going to do with it? I don't know yet, but things are looking up.

I get the news that in two weeks I have to accompany my godfather to Miami for a consultation to remove cataracts from his eyes. His failing vision makes it difficult for him to travel alone, so the job falls upon my shoulders. We'll be there for five days. Since Nia is recovering well, I think it will be okay for me to go. My children are left in the care of my parents and sisters. I am thrilled at the prospect of flying and leaving Jamaica for the first time. No one knows that I'm scared of flying. As the airplane taxis down the runway, the butterflies in my stomach almost stifle me. My knuckles are white as I hold on tightly to the armrest. The special treatment reserved for heads of government is lavished on us. We are met by important people and promptly cleared through customs security. A chauffeur meets us and we are escorted to a Rolls Royce. I wish my family could get a glimpse of me as I settle into its luxurious leather.

Our accommodations in Florida are a posh beachfront home in Boca Raton. The lavishness of the residence makes my eyes round. The beach is a few feet away from the deck, to which an unbelievable yacht is anchored. It sparkles as the sunlight dances off the water, inviting one to come on in. I fall in love with Florida, deciding then and there that one day I will live here. The times between doctor's appointments are spent cruising on the yacht, visiting friends and being entertained in all manner of ways. I get a good preview into the lives of the rich and famous.

The cataract surgery is scheduled for two months away. I shop for my family and children, returning home with a suitcase filled with clothes and toys for the children. In my absence, Jessica and Nia missed me, but their eyes are round with joy when they open all the new toys from America.

During my absence, my baby stitches came apart. My return home was not one day too soon. Nia's stomach has a gaping hole with her intestines almost spilling out of the cavity. I spend the night holding her in my arms. Her temperature is 104 degrees. I call Chad telling him of our baby's condition. My mother, while never missing an opportunity to get into everyone's life and business, had neglected to call him so he could have taken her to the hospital. He, on the other hand, assumed that since Nia was with my mother, she was being properly cared for and had not visited the children while I was out of the country. I'm too concerned about my baby to get mad at either one of them right then. I'm just praying that Nia will make it through the night.

At the hospital the following morning, she is admitted. The incision has to be sutured and her temperature brought under control. Two days later, they feel she is well enough to return home. Every day for ten days, she has to be taken to the hospital to have her wound cleaned and dressed. With tender loving care, her body heals but not without leaving an awful folding of skin and scars where a neat belly button should have been. She will never be able to wear a bikini to the beach.

Eight weeks later, I again accompany my godfather to Florida to undergo cataract surgery at the Bascom Palmer Eye Institute. We are met at the airport by the same chauffeur-driver Rolls Royce, and once again driven to the beachfront property in Boca Raton, where we remain for the two days prior to the surgery. Two days later, we are driven to Miami and booked into the Omni Hotel. I learn that if I take the elevator to the bottom floor of the hotel, there is an entire shopping mall down there. On the evening before the surgery, I leave him upstairs and take the elevator downstairs to the mall. This is paradise to a girl who is only off the Island for the second time in her

23 years. I'm strolling along, trying to look sophisticated as I browse through the stores, hoping to explore and do some shopping. I'm oblivious to the fact that I am being watched.

A young man approaches me. With a smile on his face he greets me, "Hi pretty lady."

"Hello," I reply.

"You from back home?"

"Yes, I'm from Jamaica."

"It is so good to meet someone from home. You live here?"

"No, just visiting."

"You are the right person that I want to meet, someone from home. Come here, I want to share something with you. You can't trust everybody but since we are from the same place I am going to share this with you."

I'm led to a bench and he sits down next to me. He opens the top of the brown paper bag giving me a glimpse of its contents. In a hushed voice he explains, "I just came into this unexpected fortune. I have thousands of dollars right here in this bag and have been looking for someone to share it with. I just found the right person. I know things are hard back home, and so I want to share it with you."

Warily, I ask, "Why would you do that?"

"Because I want to help someone from back home. This is how it works: You must promise not to tell anyone about this, and the only way I can trust you to do that, since I don't know you, is for you to give me $100."

"Why would I give you $100? I don't know you."

"Well, when you give me $100, I give you $5000. You lose nothing. Your up-front money is just telling me that you deserve this good fortune."

I think about it for a few minutes then ask. "How long have you been looking for someone to share this fortune with?"

"I have been here all morning. I talked with two other young ladies, but none of them was worthy to share it with me. You, on the other hand, is perfect. You are beautiful and took the time to talk with me – that makes you the person that I have been looking for." His reasoning sounds good to me, and I am flattered that he thinks I am worthy. I produce the only money I have to shop, a $100 bill, and hand it over to him.

"Okay. I don't want all these people to see me counting out all this money so let me go separate your share and bring it back to you. Stay right here, I'll be right back."

"Okay, I hope I can trust you."

"Watch the time. I'll be back in exactly ten minutes."

Two hours later I'm still sitting in the same spot, waiting for him to return with my money.

Eventually it dawns on me that I had been taken for a ride. I feel like a big fool. Angry tears sting my eyes, and I feel sick to my stomach. Looking around to see if anyone had witnessed my stupidity, I see a salesman who had wished me a good day looking at me from the doorway. Our eyes meet, and he ever so slightly shakes his head, purses his lips and retreats into the store. He had just witnessed another unsuspecting victim to a crime.

I just lost all the money I had to shop. What am I going to tell my children who are looking for gifts? With slumped shoulders I take the elevator back upstairs Uncle Nowington hears me coming in the door, and asks, "How was your shopping?"

"I'll go back tomorrow. I just wanted to see what was available downstairs," I reply.

Chapter Twelve

FREEDOM FROM MOTHER

I t is time for Lynnette's children to migrate to Canada. They will be missed, but they need their mother. As the day of their departure approaches, we spend as much time as possible with them, knowing that when they leave, we have no idea when we we'll see them again. We seem to be losing our family to Canada. The country has now claimed seven of my family members.

My parents' house is strangely quiet without my nieces and nephew. I dream of the day when I too will leave the shores of Jamaica for a brighter future. Working for my godfather continues. His raping has stopped since the St. Thomas episode, and although my life is beginning to take on some form of normalcy, I still harbor great resentment towards him. Going to work daily is a chore, but it has its benefits. I don't have to struggle on the bus to get to work, and when I need to take care of my children's illnesses, it's never a problem if Chad is unavailable to take us to the doctor or hospital – the chauffeured car is always available.

Janice has completed college and is employed at a private school, attended almost exclusively by the children of the country's dignitaries. She enrolls Jessica there and takes her in the mornings. Tuition is quite expensive, but my daughter attends for free. She is receiving a good basic education and plays with the children of the crème de la crème; all for free. Mama continues caring for Nia during the days.

Lester, my brother, introduces an attractive young lady named Kelly to the family. The two are very much in love and have been living together. Mama hates her, swearing to do everything in her power to break them up. Kelly falls in love with Jessica on their first meeting. She begins expressing a desire for a little girl just like Jessica. Her love for my child becomes an obsession, causing me to carefully watch her every movement on her frequent visits. Six months later, she gleefully announces her pregnancy with what she hope will be a little girl just like Jessica.

As the pregnancy progresses she becomes very ill. Her morning sickness is almost debilitating, and instead of gaining weight she begins losing it. Her doctor becomes concerned and run tests. To everyone's dismay, she is diagnosed with leukemia. Lester is devastated, and Kelly is terrified. What will be the outcome of the pregnancy?

Mama is convinced that God is punishing Kelly for what she calls her insolence. She has been one of the few people who is not intimidated by Mama – instead she stands up to her unreasonable demands, defending herself against the verbal abuse and lies she tells Lester about her. Returning home with the smugness of a cat that had gotten the cream, Mama proudly recounts her latest encounter with Kelly. She showed up at their apartment unannounced. Without knocking, she walks in the unlocked door, which Kelly leaves that way in case of emergencies. Following sounds she finds Kelly huddled on the bathroom floor, hugging the commode. Kelly is relieved that someone has come to help her. She stretches up her hand begging to be helped up from the floor.

Mama laughs in the face of the one prostrate before her, telling her that God has finally avenged her for all the times she had been rude to her. She tells her that seeing her in that position, helpless and begging, is the best revenge she could have asked for. Mama then turns on her heels leaving on the bathroom floor the mother of her son's unborn child, a woman who has terminal cancer.

A couple weeks later she is hospitalized. She has been unable to digest food to sustain herself and her growing baby. The doctors prescribe complete bed rest and a special diet. The special diet and bed rest achieves nothing. She continues experiencing violent episodes of illnesses. In the fifth month of her pregnancy she is hospitalized again, where she will remain until she gives birth. Her prognosis is terminal. All they can do for her now is keep her hospitalized to give the baby a fighting chance. She is expected to die as soon as she delivers her baby.

Lester is inconsolable. We pray and hope for a change in the prognosis. None comes. During the seventh month, it's clear that her demise is imminent. The vivacious young lady, whom we have come to know and love, who had fallen head over heels in love with my daughter, has been reduced to a skeleton. Bare bones and a small lump of a stomach are the only proof that a life is clinging on inside of her – the only indication of what is to be. She barely recognizes us, as she exists between reality and a drug-induced stupor.

Hugging the skeletal frame almost lost within the folds of white sheets, it is painfully apparent that this is the last time I will see her. Lester regrets the pregnancy, believing that if she had not gotten pregnant she would at least have had a fighting chance at survival.

The following day, Lester gives us the sad news that the baby has been delivered by caesarian section, but Kelly has lost her fight with leukemia. One life had come into the world at the expense of another. Lester has gained a daughter, but has lost the love of his life.

With members of both families at his side, Lester buries Kelly. Then he takes home his baby daughter, whom he names Crystal. He is heartbroken, but there is little time to lie down and grieve. Crystal has to be cared for. A side effect of the immense amount of drugs administered to her mother, Crystal suffers health problems of her own. She appears to be a little slow in her mental development. She walks late, talks late; she potty trains late, and displays problems with retention of simple instructions. She has trouble with basic aptitudes and memorizing the alphabet.

Concerned for her future, and worried that the lack of programs to help Crystal develop into a high-functioning young lady will not be available either from Lester or from the Jamaican Government, Amelia and Lester decide that the best thing for Crystal will be for her to be adopted by his sister and given a new life in Canada.

Mama is invited to accompany four-year-old Crystal on the trip to Canada, she is also invited to remain in Canada with Amelia for an extended period. She accepts the invitation. The idea that she will be out of our lives even for a short time is exhilarating. The years have done nothing to mellow her into a nice person. We have matured to the point where she has been unable to exert total control over our lives, but she is still a force to be reckoned with. Daddy tried his best to remain at home but had not been able to. One morning, in a fit of rage she threw his beloved keyboard, along with all his belongings out the door, kicking him out right behind them. Daddy, after raising all these children, has found himself alone, in a rented room fending for himself. Her impending departure is good news. She will not be missed.

Conversation with Mama has been limited to the affairs of my children. I am therefore surprised when she asks to speak with me one evening, as I gather my daughters to take them home. Curiosity gets the better of me, and I sit down to listen.

"You know that Amelia has adopted Crystal and she will be going to Canada to live with her?"

"Yes I know. That was nice of Amelia, because Crystal is going to need special care, and there is none here to care for her properly."

"Yes, but more than that, she has asked me to bring up Crystal and remain there with her for a vacation."

"That's a good thing. You need a vacation. How long will you be gone?"

"That's why I need to talk to you. My visa is for five years and Amelia says I can stay for about two years, come back for a few months and return again."

"That sounds good."

"It sounds good, but I can't just leave Cheryl in the house with Anton. Janice and Bridget are here, but they are all still young. So I have been wondering if you would be willing to move back in here to take care of the children and provide adult supervision while I'm gone."

I'm flabbergasted. She has actually invited me back into her home and even called me an adult. I listen to the proposal, and promise to discuss it with Chad. I relate the story to my sisters and they love the idea. The prospect of all of us living together again is exciting.

Chad is not crazy about the idea of my giving up the apartment and moving back into my parent's home. We won't be able to continue living together under the new arrangements. He allows me to make my own decision. Although I enjoy being with him, the prospect of a long-term relationship culminating in marriage is still uncertain. After lengthy discussions, I accept the offer to move back home. Chad returns to his Mama, and my brother, Leroy, decides to take over the apartment.

To the airport we go, carrying mother and Crystal to board their flight to Canada. From the gallery we wave goodbye. The anticipation of a home without her is overwhelming. Around us, on the waving gallery others are crying for heir loved ones – they must think we are crazy because we are all smiles and laughter. For the first time in our lives, we will be free from Mother's wrath. Not a tear is shed at her departure. We return home from the airport and throw the first party ever held in the home. We talk and laugh freely, staying up late watching television. We are free from her iron hand.

Living on my own with my two children has had its hardships. After paying the mortgage, utilities and food, very little is left for anything else. Uncle Nowington is wealthy, but I ask for nothing – in his opinion I am being paid a good salary, so I leave it at that. My sisters often assist with groceries and Janice takes great pleasure in shopping for her nieces. They are the most beautiful and best-dressed little girls in the community.

Returning home is the beginning of the end of the relationship between Chad and me. Over time, he visits less frequently. Until now, he has seen the children only when I take them to visit him at his mother's home. By this time, Jessica's father has remarried. He had asked for my hand in marriage three times, always receiving no for an answer. He has moved on with his life, leaving his daughter behind. He's providing no financial support, and we fare no better with Chad. I'm raising my children on my own. But life isn't so hard. Three of us work, so with our pooled resources, the benefits of working for one common goal is easier.

My girls are five and two years old. Janice is now teaching at a high school, and Jessica has been registered in Holy Childhood Preparatory School, a private school costing more than I can afford per term. Providing a solid education for my children is very important to me, so making the sacrifice is well worth the effort. Nia and Nadine are in kindergarten together. My girls enjoy living in a household of aunts, uncles, and cousins; there is no shortage of hands to hold, arms to hug and cheeks to kiss.

They lack nothing. We lavish so much on them they become just a little pampered. Jessica receives a cute puppy from a friend. We name him Bruno. The puppy grows into a huge German shepherd, jumping over chairs and knocking the girls off their feet. We love Bruno, but Jessica is petrified of him due to his sheer size.

One Sunday evening, I take the girls to visit Chad' mother. Nia is playing inside while Jessica explores the front yard. Out of nowhere, a dog appears. Jessica catches a glimpse of him and begins running into the house. The dog, sensing her fear, lunges at her, grabbing hold of her dress as she dashes for the door. Her screams bring us running outside. Attached to the hem of her dress is a dog refusing to let go. We run to help her. The sight and the look of terror on her face is frightening. Grabbing a broom, I beat the dog until he releases my daughter's dress. This episode has done nothing to alleviate Jessica's fear of dogs. She is horrified of them. By the time the dog loosens his grip on her dress, she is practically naked, as he has torn the dress off from the waist. There is no consoling her, so we go home. This ends the visits to Chad's mother: Jessica refuses to return.

Bridget is teaching at our alma mater. She becomes pregnant, and after a difficult pregnancy and a caesarian delivery, she has a baby boy named Andrew. He is a quiet child, growing into a very intelligent boy. He loves his mother above all others. Bridget is known for her lack of culinary skills but Andrew bravely eats whatever she prepares. Even when everyone knows the meal tastes disgusting, he chews, wincing in agony, swallowing each offending morsel. But he always thanks his mom for a delicious meal. He is a sweetheart.

Uncle Nowington has to pay another visit to Florida. Again I'm his designated traveling companion. We will be leaving on Monday. Sunday afternoon I'm walking home from visiting a friend. A car slows down by my side as it approaches me. Slowing my steps I look at the unfamiliar driver. The car stops next to me and the driver leans out to speak to me. Ahh, I know who it is, it's the owner of a farmers' market where I do my weekly shopping. He introduces himself.

"Hi. Thought it was you. Can I give you a ride to where you are going?"

"Hi there," I reply. "thanks, but I'm almost home."

"Do you live around here?"

"Yes. Do you?"

"No I'm taking a short cut through here to Pembroke Hall, where I live." As he extends his hand.

"By the way my name is Norris O'Connor. You come into the store every week, but I have no idea who you are. What's your name, pretty lady?"

"I'm Marcia."

"Hello Marcia. I must tell you that you are a beautiful lady. I like you and have been waiting for an opportunity to ask you out. Are you married?"

"Thank you. No, I'm not married."

"Good," he smiles. "Can I take you out for dinner and a little dancing tonight?"

"I would love to go but I'm leaving for Florida early tomorrow morning and need to pack."

"Oh man, just my luck. After all this time, as soon as I get to talk to you, you are leaving for America."

"I'll only be gone for ten days."

"That's what you say," he replies. "No one who goes to America ever comes back, so I guess it's hello and goodbye."

"Not me. This is my third visit to Florida. I'll be back and as soon as I return, I'll come to the store," I assure him.

"Promise?"

"I promise. Take care!"

The trip to Florida is completed without incident, business is accomplished and we return home to resume life as normal. A few days later, I visit the farmers market to purchase supplies and Norris is immediately at my side. He tells me how glad he is to see me, confessing he had doubts that I would have returned from the USA. "I have no intention of leaving Jamaica, at least not yet."

The following Friday I'm back in the store. Norris' face lights up when he sees me. We talk for a while, exchanging telephone numbers. Later that night he calls me, inviting me to dinner and a movie on Saturday night. I refuse the offer, telling him I didn't know him and do not trust strangers.

On Sunday he calls again, asking for an invitation to my home so we can talk, and get to know each other. I give him my address, and he shows up. He meets the family. We talk for about two hours. As the following weekend approaches, he invites me to a barbecue at his cousin's home in Red Hills. He promises to return me safely. I accept the invitation.

His family and friends welcome me into their midst and before long I have a bottle of beer in my hand, I'm laughing at their jokes, and talking up a storm, When it's time for us to leave, Norris assures them that they will be seeing much more of me.

Driving home he suggests stopping at a nightclub.

"My favorite club is right down the street. Its owned by a friend of mine. Do you mind if we stop for a drink?" he asks.

"I don't want to go to a club," I tell him. "Can you just take me home?"

"Come on, don't be a spoiled sport. We had a good afternoon let's finish it off with a drink."

"Okay, but not for too long, I want to go home."

"I promise not to keep you out too late. I don't want to make you mad at me and not go out with me again. We'll only stay one hour."

Before long, he has me on the dance floor pleading for just one dance. We dance to one song, two songs, then to three. Before long it's two hours. Glancing at the time I become adamant about going home. He reluctantly obliges.

At the door I'm met by one of my sisters telling me that I'm in trouble.

"What have I done to be in trouble?"

Chad came by to take you out. Daddy, who was visiting us for the day, told him you were out on a date. He got upset and left in a huff."

It has been months since he showed any interest in either Nia or me. Tough luck if his feathers have been ruffled; I no longer care. With Mama in Canada, Daddy has moved back home. It's good having him back.

Soon Norris and I are going out weekly. On Friday evenings as soon as he closes his business, he comes right over to my home.

Always in the back of his car is a box; laden with meat, vegetables, fruits, and other items from his store, and hidden somewhere in the box are treats for the three girls. He often takes them to the ice cream parlor treating them to whatever they want.

He reveals to me that he has been married, and has three sons. Although still married, the union has been broken and they have been living separately for ten years. She lives in New York with two of their sons; the eldest still resides in Jamaica. He has assured me that the marriage have been over for years, explaining several incidents which led to the breakup of the union. The different views and way of discipline administered to the children have been a major factor in their frequent arguments and disagreements, which ultimately led to the years of separation. I sympathized with him over the loss of his family, but am careful never to encourage him to make the separation final with divorce. If that is to be done, it should be his decision alone.

There is no need to look long to see that Norris is a much older man than I am. I have not asked his age, summarizing that he may be in his 30s. He has taken on the task of teaching me to dance, and the art of consuming alcohol. The lessons begin with gin and tonic. I get accustomed to the strange taste, liking it. I love the feeling of excitement and exhilaration it gives me. Soon I graduate from gin and tonic to vodka and orange juice. I'm a good student, excelling in the sadistic and addictive act of "holding my liquor." With great pride, I graduate to scotch on the rocks.

Scotch, especially undiluted with anything except the melting ice, is a little harder to swallow, but under his skillful hands I'm soon able to "drink any man under the table." My capacity to tolerate the consumption of large amounts of alcohol frightens me, but those thoughts are quickly pushed to the back of my mind as I drink and dance, swaying to music every weekend. The term "designated driver" has never been heard of, but someone surely needs to be designated to drive, as we leave the clubs early Saturday and Sunday mornings at times weaving down the streets throwing our heads back in uncontrollable mirth as he drives me home. But it's fun; I'm slowly becoming addicted to this new-found freedom.

My children now see very little of me on the weekends. After coming home late on Friday and Saturday nights, I try spending time with them on Sunday, but the hangover from the previous night's drinking keeps me in a fog. Then almost as soon as I revive to the point of being able to meet their needs, Norris shows up again ready to whisk me off to another playground. When I refuse, citing the need to do the children's laundry or prepare meals, he quickly asks what the cost would be for my sisters to do the chores for me. My sisters in turn, gladly state a price, and I'm free to go. Jessica begins resenting this new intrusion in her life, robbing her of my presence. The trips to the ice cream parlor are no longer enjoyable for her. She flatly refuses to be placated with any treats from him.

On more than one occasion, my sisters have plans of their own, leaving us with no adult supervision for the girls. My need to get out is so great that I take the children to Chad's mother. Jessica is still afraid to be there, and she hangs on to me crying, begging me not to leave her. But I kiss her, gently remove her fingers from my clothing, and we are off, leaving the children in the care of Chad's mother while we head off to some event, or simply to meet friends as we bar hop around town.

We go as far as the west coast: Montego Bay, Negril, St. Catherine, Spanish Town, St. Ann's Bay. There's no telling where our travels will take us on any given Sunday. Wherever the party is, we find it. One Sunday afternoon we stop to get something to eat. Instead of ordering jerk chicken for me as usual, he places two orders of jerk pork. Without much cajoling I'm eating. Never before in my life have I raised a morsel of this forbidden flesh to my lips. Chewing on it, all the teachings from our parents and from church rush into my memory. I almost choke on the pork, but I ignore all the warnings. Watching me, he gloats, saying. "I got the Seventh-day Adventist to eat pork. Tell me that's not the sweetest meat you have ever eaten."

My family knows about my drinking escapades, but not one word will be uttered about the consumption of swine's flesh. I have ventured into unchartered waters, and no matter how loving and supportive my family is, this cannot be told. They will not understand. I have broken all the rules of my parents and what used to be my religion, and no one has ventured out this far into the unknown. I'm ashamed to admit it.

136

Before our mother's departure to Canada, all the other children, with the exception of Anthon, have stopped attending church. With maturity came rebellion. We rebelled against our mother's treatment of us, her betrayal of our trust to protect us from danger and abuse, her treatment of our father and of strangers. As the children mature, regardless of what she threatens or does, attending church is no longer an option for us. We simply refuse to go.

Norris proudly announces to his friends his great accomplishment in getting the Seventh-day Adventist to eat pork, drink alcohol and dance the nights away. I cringe inside. I'm ashamed of some of my actions, but it's too late. There is no going back now. I had become a pork-eating, liquor-drinking, backsliding Seventh-day Adventist. This is now a part of our weekly routine. Sometimes I request jerk chicken, but Norris tells me to stop pretending to dislike his favorite meat. It is good and I know it. There is no arguing the matter. Secretly, I consume jerk pork every Sunday, followed by a drink to rid my taste buds of the memory.

Three months after our first date, he takes me to his home. I'm genuinely surprise at the state of the house. He lives in an upper middle-class neighborhood, which doesn't surprise me. He's giving me the grand tour and the master bedroom grabs my attention. It seems as if the woman of the house had recently left for work, expecting to return any minute. Her perfumes, make-up and personal items are all neatly lined up on the dresser. Her clothes are neatly hanging in the closet, and a variety of shoes stand ready to be stepped into. The feeling of invading another woman's private space is overwhelming, almost as if her presence is lingering at the door watching me.

I ask him why he keeps her belongings in such pristine condition if she left ten years ago. He explains that he doesn't sleep in the room, but in another bedroom, which he calls his music room, therefore he has no reason to disturb her stuff. This explanation sounds plausible and I accept it. The house tour ends and we sit down in the living room to talk. A few minutes later, there is a loud knock at the gate and the three fierce German shepherd dogs in the backyard start barking ferociously.

Norris goes out the door to see what the commotion is all about. Within a few seconds, I hear loud angry voices outside. I hear a woman yelling. Curiosity gets the better of me and I peek out the window. From my vantage point, I see and hear her making demands to come in. She is yelling that she knows he has been seeing another woman who is inside the house.

"I know that you have a woman in there. For months now you have been very evasive, I can't reach you on the telephone and you are never home. What's going on?"

"Margie, I'm telling you again go home. What I do is none of your business, I'm my own big man."

"It is my business. You have been telling me you love me, and I have put my life on hold for you. Now you're seeing someone else. I want to see her so I can tell her who you really are. Let me in now."

"If you come in here and the dogs bite you it's your problem. Go home and I'll talk to you tomorrow."

"I don't want to talk to you tomorrow. You are a lying, two-timing bastard and I hope she finds that out before she gets hurt the way you have hurt me. This is not over. If you think you can get rid of me just like this, you are wrong. I'm going to get back at you, you'll see."

With the dogs barking and her yelling, neighbors are peeking from behind their curtains. Still yelling about him being a two-timing bastard, she walks away. Norris watches her walk away, waiting until she disappears around the corner.

A thousand questions race through my mind. I want answers. He tries assuring me that there is nothing between them except for a newly formed friendship.

"Do you think I'm stupid? If there is nothing going on between both of you why is she be so angry at you for what she thinks is going on?"

"Honestly, there is nothing going on. We met a few weeks before I met you. We went out for drinks a couple times. We have never been intimate and I don't know why she would come here saying all those things."

"Women do not behave like that unless you give them a reason to do so. You must have made promises to her or lied to her. Which one is it?"

"Neither. Whatever she thinks I told her is all in her head. If I wanted to be with her, I would have been. Don't let her ruin the afternoon. Forget about her, this won't happen again.

One month later he tells me that he has to make a trip to Miami for business. I don't know what type of business he has in Miami, and refrain from asking too many questions. He discloses that he is a United States resident, which requires him to make yearly trips to keep his status. He claims that on those trips, he shops for clothes and other items. The day of his departure, he picks me up from work taking me to his home. He needs help packing his bags. He's in the shower and I am folding his clothes and packing his suitcase for him. I notice his passport lying on the bed. Picking it up I read his information. He is who he says he is. I look for his birth date; it jumps off the page at me. I blink my eyes looking again. Are my eyes playing tricks on me? Are my eyes sending the correct information to my brain? Looking again I focus on the year - 1933. He was born in1933. How old does that make him?

I do the math, but I refuse to believe the answer. When I hear the shower turned off I return the passport to its place and continue packing his bags. But my mind is consumed with this information.

He could not be that old. His brother comes to take him to the airport and we secured the home, leaving the dogs in the care of a family friend. On the way to the airport, they drop me off at my home. Immediately I grab paper and pencil doing the math again. No, it still has to be incorrect. I ask my sisters to do the calculation and they give me the same answer. I have been going out with a man who is twice my age. I'm 24 years old and he is 48. He could easily be my father. I'm thrown into frenzy. What should I do when he returns in a couple weeks? What am I going to do then? Should I continue seeing him?

With Norris gone, I spend my weekends with my girls. They are happy to have me back to themselves. I had become so consumed with having a good time, that the children had been neglected. Trekking all over the Island had blinded my eyes to their needs. They are growing up so fast, we need to relish every moment with them. We take them to the zoo, the botanical garden, to the beach and to the movies.

Two weeks later, Norris returns from Miami. He drops his bags off at his home and makes a beeline to mine. We are happy to see him back. He had become a regular visitor, even playing board games with us at times. I think he misses his family and receives some sort of satisfaction being with us. I decide to leave the age issue alone. At least; for now.

Our friendship resumes, but I curtail my absence from my home. Instead of being gone every weekend I go out twice per month, spending more time with the children as promised. We fall into a comfortable routine. As the months pass by we're acutely aware that the time for our mother's return from Canada is fast approaching. I have not decided whether to resume living in the apartment or find a new place. What I do know is that as soon as she returns, I'm out of here.

The mailman delivers the letter containing the dreaded news. Mama will be returning home in six weeks.

TEN

Chapter Thirteen

MOTHER'S WRATH

Mama's imminent return will drastically change our lives. For two years, we have experienced total freedom, and it's about to be yanked away. The harmony and bliss will be replaced with tension, stress, fighting, yelling and verbal abuse. All negative. There is nothing positive about her. Why does she have to come back? We are not looking forward to her return. But regardless of what we think or how we feel, the date is fast approaching and adjustments must be made.

Cheryl has formed a relationship with a young man in the neighborhood named Malik. He loves her daughter, Nadine, frequently visiting to play and bring her treats. A wholesome atmosphere exists. We tell Norris and Malik about our mother's impending return from Canada. Malik, being from the neighborhood, knows her, but Norris had never had the privilege of making her acquaintance. This prospect scares me. But there is no avoiding the reality of the situation. They will have to be introduced. The dreaded day draws closer. Oh God, it's today. Norris graciously agrees to give me a ride to the airport to pick her up. With great trepidation I wait for the time to leave home to make the trip. It's as if a gloom of death has been cast over the household. Such a great contrast exists between her departure and her return. If I had control over the sun, this day would never have dawned.

Reluctantly, we leave for the airport. There is no joy in my heart. I struggle to tell Norris about her disposition, without divulging family secrets. He has a difficult time understanding what I'm trying to tell him. After all, most people love their mothers and miss them when they are absent. He thinks I should be ecstatic at her return. But he doesn't know and cannot comprehend the family dynamics.

Air Canada arrives on schedule. I hope against hope that she had missed the flight in Toronto, but am not that lucky. My heart sinks when, as the passengers claim their luggage, I see her. Pointing her out to Norris, I plaster a smile on my face as she approaches us. We greet and hug. She looks good, and it seems that she enjoyed her extended vacation. I wish she had made a permanent change of address, but how could I wish this awful fate upon my sisters and their households in Canada?

She emerges from customs into the open pick-up area. We greet each other with a hug. I introduced her to Norris who receives a cold stare; she barely acknowledges his presence. Embarrassment washes over me. We load her luggage in the car and begin the drive home. An awkward silence permeates the car. Several times I try to break the ice, but I'm not having much success. After a while she starts talking about the wonderful time spent in Canada. She announces her regret having to return to Jamaica. She also confides to us that she had asked her daughters to allow her to remain in Canada, but was told by them that they treasure their relationship, and her being there permanently would put too much pressure on the relationship. Her stay had therefore come to an end. Now she is back in Jamaica. Lucky us.

This is her home, so I am in no position to turn her away. If I don't like her rules, I can leave. I have survived childhood, becoming a self-sufficient adult. Listening to her recount her stay in Canada brings a smile to my face. From her point of view, it was perfectly idyllic.

At home, the rest of the gang has done a great job making the house appear welcoming for her. We had cooked a meal, and cleaned the house until it shone. Hopefully, she'll find nothing to complain about. The car pulls up at the gate and her grandchildren run out to greet her, as Norris and I carry in her bags. The others paint smiles on their faces, mustering up their courage to make the approach. We succeed in making her feel welcome as she struts into her domain to resume ruling with what had been an iron hand.

We politely listen to her escapades. She tells us about the wonderful places she had visited. The vastness of the foreign land, the six-lane highways where cars sped along at the unbelievable speed of 65 miles per hour. She elaborates about the beautiful homes of our sisters. The bone-chilling cold of winter, snow piled as high as the covered cars, and the searing heat of summer. She tells of the beautiful snow-capped mountains and snow-laden trees. Of Niagara Falls in all its glory, as it cascades down the rocks, emptying itself into the lake. We are genuinely happy that she had been given such a wonderful opportunity to get off the island, visit new places, and enjoy new experiences.

But as usual, her pleasantries are short-lived. Her story telling comes to an end. And she inquires about our welfare. We assure her that we are well. She turns her attention to me, then to Norris. "And who would this gentleman be?" she asks.

"He is a very good friend of mine."

To the total astonishment of everyone in the room, my mother looks at the man she had recently met, saying to him, "Be careful of your friendship and your feelings for her, because she changes men as often as you change your socks."

Absolute humiliation. Total embarrassment. Unbelievable shame. Hate, loathing and fury seethes through my body. I shiver from head to toe and back again, causing angry tears to sting my eyes. Goose pimples rise on my flesh, adrenalin pumps through my veins and my lips tremble with anger. For the second time in my life, because of her, I wish the ground would open up and swallow me. My concern is for Norris. What is he thinking? How will he react? What will be his decision regarding me after hearing this from my own mother?

The air is so thick with apprehension it can be cut with a knife. Looks of shock dumfound my sisters as they all look at me with pity in their eyes. I open my mouth to offer some unknown explanation to Norris, but sensing my discomfort and seeing my pain he takes my hand in his. "It's okay, you don't have to explain anything. I'll go now, we'll talk later."

I walk him to his car, trying to explain why she would make such a remark, making excuses for my mother. He simply assured me. "It is all right, forget about it. What she said does not change how I feel about you." Promising to speak with me the next day, he leaves. I'm so angry with her. Nothing hidden in the bags interests me; I walk away seeking refuge in my old room. This is the clincher. My answer is clear. I definitely will not be remaining here now that she is back.

There is no normalcy for life to return to. When a prisoner has been given his freedom, it is awfully foolish of him to voluntarily return to captivity. I need a new apartment. Moving day is imminent. Mama tries exerting her control over us again, but too much has happened during the time she had been gone. Even so, some respect must be shown to her, so we adjust ourselves and try falling back into stride. It's not easy. The one thing, which will absolutely not happen is for us to attend church. Anthon has continued going, but the rest of us want no part of her religion or her God.

Conflicts arise daily between us. We literally rub each other the wrong way. She is critical of everything I do, from the way I indulge or discipline my children, to the fact that I am going out with an older man. She disapproves of my weekend outings and complains bitterly if my sisters are not home and the children are left with her. In an effort to alleviate the pressure, I curtail my outings. She develops a love/hate attraction to Norris. In his presence she drips with honey, while in his absence she turns the dagger in his back. She constantly tells me he's only using me, that I am only an old man's past time.

Usually I ignore her, but one day her comments are so blistering that I have to say something. "You are just jealous because someone likes me. You hate me because you have become a has-been, and I am young, beautiful, and have the world at my feet."

"You think you're all that. It is only because of me that any of you are here, and I can still take out any one of you that I choose. Go on, keep thinking that all is well, when you think it's all peace and safety there is going to be sudden destruction."

She has never been short on unpleasant surprises. She is as unpredictable and unstable as the waves of the ocean. No one knows when or where she will rise up or come crashing down upon your head. Life with her has regained its hellish qualities. I must get out of her house.

It's Sunday afternoon and Norris is coming to pick me up to attend a party with him. My sisters have agreed to care for my girls.

Just before Norris arrives Mama disappears upstairs. I have no idea what she's up to. Norris comes in, greets the girls – handing over candy and treats. We hear Mama's voice at the top of the stairs. Our eyes turn upwards. To our great astonishment, there at the top of the stairs, poised in the flirtatious stance of a stripper stands my mother wearing the shortest shorts and midriff blouse of a teenager.

"Norris," she utters in a coy tone, "Why would you want her, when you can have me? She has no idea how to please a man like you. I can take you to places you have never been to, and make you feel the way you deserve to feel."

Is there no end to this woman?

With mouths gaping we look up at her in disbelief. Her 57-year-old body that has borne 15 children sashays down the stairs. Fluttering her eyes at him, she sensuously rubs her hands over her sagging, stretch-marked, distended stomach. We look at her fried-eggs flat breast, barely concealed by the skimpy shirt, her lumpy cellulite-packed legs, and huge hips pushing against the too-tight shorts she has no business wearing. The sight of her is disgusting.

"Mama what are you doing? Go back upstairs and put some clothes on." She ignores me presenting herself in front of Norris. She repeats her question.

"She is just a girl. Why would you want her instead of me? She has no idea how to please a man."

Norris smiles at her with pity in his eyes.

I want to kill her. Hateful thoughts and ways to get rid of her race through my mind. "Norris let's go," I manage to mutter. Throwing her a look filled with venom, we walk out the door. She watches from the doorway as he opens the passenger door for me to get in, and then slams her door. I'm in tears as soon as the door closes. What can I say to him? How do I explain away the behavior of my mother? Should I tell him that she has a mental problem? Maybe that will explain her erratic behavior. Or should I just tell him how she has been trying to kill me since birth. What would he do if I told him how she had sold me to Uncle Nowington for years? Will he understand any of it? Will he still want to be with me if he knew the truth about my life? She has not succeeded in killing me, and has now embarked upon a crusade to ruin my life.

None of my thoughts are expressed. Silent and sullen, I sit in his car. "Your mother is just a little jealous that you girls are having a good time. She probably had a hard life when she was this age. Don't worry about it and don't take it so seriously. She is just having some fun." If he only knew how much I need to worry about it. This is no fun: all-out war has just been declared between us. If she was going to begin making passes at Norris, then mother and daughter have entered a new phase in our relationship. She has her husband. Daddy is very much alive and well. I guess the prospect of a younger man entices her. Well, she is not going to win this war. I decide then and there to remain in her home, flaunt my relationship in her face and watch her make a fool of herself. Two can play at that game.

Making myself more available to Norris increases my absence from home. Now the partying begins on Friday nights. We meet friends at designated places to eat roast fish, drink beer and alcohol and jam to reggae music. I sleep most of Saturday; get up to care for the girls, leaving later to dance and drink the night away at a nightclub. Sunday afternoons are spent visiting friends and drinking more alcohol. This is now my weekly routine. Mother's objections to my life style fall on deaf ears. What she says or does means absolutely nothing to me.

I'm out of control. Defiance is my main objective. Rebellion against everything she pretends to stand for runs hot in my veins. I talk about our relationship within her hearing, caring not one bit about what she says. One Friday night after the usual reveling, Norris takes me home. My key turns in the lock but the door remains locked; pushing at it I realize that another lock has been added. I knock. One of my sisters comes to unlock the door. Mother threatens her with death if she dares to open it. Norris is sitting in his car watching and waiting to see me safely enter the house. Realizing I have a problem he gets out of his car to help. From her upstairs bedroom window she yells. "Get away from my door you little slut, I don't want you in my house. Go back where you are coming from." Looking up at her in the window I reply.

"That's no problem, I'll gladly go back." I walk out the gate and back into the car. Norris takes me home with him. This begins a new phase of our relationship.

146

The Odyssey Of Survival

When I return home Saturday afternoon she calls me every name in the book. I wonder aloud what pastor had preached at church earlier. She scorns me for what she assumes had taken place in Norris's bed. She provided that opportunity by locking me out of the house. I'm certainly not about to sleep under the stars. I had a very enjoyable night and nothing she says will erase the smile from my face. If she locks me out again I know where another bed waits to welcome me. As a matter of fact I will personally take every opportunity to return to his bed.

Eventually she learns to ignore me, even feigning blindness to my existence. For my children's sake, I make adjustments to my lifestyle, paying more attention to their needs than to my mother's disapproval of me.

I don't know how, but she finds out where Norris operates his business, his address and his martial status. Mother taunts me daily about my involvement with a married man. I try explaining the years of separation to her, but she won't listen. "He is not divorced and therefore he is still a married man. It wasn't so long ago that another married man's wife tried to kill you. This time I will personally deliver you to his wife to beat the skin off your black ass."

"They are not together. She lives in America and they have been separated for ten years."

"Believe that if you want to. Tell him to make a honorable woman out of you and marry you. You already have two children for two different men, is this the way you plan to live the rest of your life?"

Norris makes another visit to Miami. She overhears me telling my sisters where he went and jumps right in.

"See what I told you, he's gone to visit his wife in America leaving you here to feed his dogs."

I'm not feeding his dogs, but her words make me wonder whether or not he has been telling me the truth about his situation. I vow to find out as soon as he returns.

He returns and I ask no questions – if anything we become inseparable. The girls love him, even Jessica has warmed up to him, and my sisters think he's wonderful. His age is a non-issue, except to my mother. She constantly refers to it, and I lend a deaf ear. She has a problem with every man I speak with. She not only hates me, but

147

also resents anyone who shows interest in me. It will be her greatest joy if I remain an unattached, unsuccessful, unmarried, uneducated, dependent individual, groveling like a dog in the trenches for the scraps falling from the table, so she can kick me around and spit in my face. My efforts to succeed or form relationships only serve to anger her. She finds every way imaginable and unimaginable to embarrass me and destroy my friendships. Especially if the relationship is with a member of the opposite sex.

Cheryl has become friendly with Malik, and their friendship has progresses to the next level. They are in love with each other. He adores her daughter. Nadine calls him Daddy. They are talking about getting married.

Mother know about their relationship, and for the most part consents to it. Malik does the right thing; he comes to the house with a plan in mind. Sitting down with her he professes his love for Cheryl, asking for her hand in marriage. She gives her approval and blessing. Excitement fills the house. We have a wedding to plan.

The engagement party is scheduled for a Saturday evening, two weeks later at Malik's home. I tell Norris about the party, but don't invite him. Everything is in place for a good time. Our little sister is going to get married and she has the support of the family. Or so we think.

The party will begin at 5pm. Malik arrives at 4:30pm to pick up Cheryl. He has no idea the trauma that Cheryl and the rest of the household have been experiencing for the last couple hours. At about 3:00pm, Mama announced that over her dead body, Cheryl was not leaving the house to go any place, especially not to attend her own engagement party. We look from one to the other trying to figure out what has happened to bring about this strange reaction. We try our hardest to get an answer from her about why the sudden turn in her mood, but she offers no explanation for her irrational decision. To make matters worse, she announces that none of us will be allowed to leave the house. Not one of us was going to be allowed out the door. At first we laugh, commenting on how crazy she is. Soon we realize that this is no laughing matter.

Frantically, I try reasoning with her to just allow Cheryl to go. Guests are waiting to share in her joy. A lot of money has been spent for the occasion, but she adamantly refuses to listen to reason. I don't know exactly what happened to trigger this behavior. I do know that we are treading on very dangerous ground. She has not only forbidden any of us to leave the house, but with a sharpened machete across her knees, she places herself in a chair by the door. Locking the door, she removes the key from the lock. With a glazed look in her eyes she dares anyone of us to attempt taking the key from her. Losing a limb or a life will be a sure thing.

We plea, beg and yell. Cheryl cries. The children get upset and they start crying. The dog is barking and we are yelling. She ignores all of us. The engagement party will go on without the fiancée. This evening, without a shadow of a doubt, we come to the realization that what we have joked about all our lives is a reality. Our mother is truly crazy.

Malik is coming through the gate, and she shouts at him through the window. "Malik do not come any further. If you take one more step into my yard I will kill you."

In astonishment and confusion he stops in his tracks. "What's going on? I'm here to get Cheryl for the party."

"Why you are here is of no concern to me. Get off my property before I have you arrested for trespassing." He presses on, telling her that the party needs to get started, almost all the guests have arrived, and everyone is waiting for Cheryl to get there.

"For the last time I am telling you to get off my property. There will be no engagement party tonight or any other night for as long as I live. Cheryl is going nowhere with you. If she leaves this house tonight, I will kill her and you. Now get out of my yard and don't come back."

Malik is bewildered. What has gone wrong? Cheryl approaches the window. Mother comes up behind her shoving her away, pulling the curtain closed.

By now the neighbors, hearing raised voices, begin gathering on the street to see what was going on. Malik starts talking with the nextdoor neighbor about our mother's behavior. The neighbor offers to try talking to her and comes through the gate. "Miss Mac what's going on? Why are you refusing to let the young people get engaged? Come out here so we can talk." Flinging the window open she yells. "You people are going to let me commit murder tonight.

Miss Lewis go home and stay out of my business, and you boy, go home to your mother."

Inside the house we group together, devising a plan to surprise her from behind, yanking the machete away from her, then grabbing the key. One at a time we get close to her, taking up our positions on opposite sides. She senses our intentions and raises the machete above her head wildly spinning around, chopping at any and everything within reach. None of us want to be killed by an insane person, so we abort the plan. Helplessly we watch as she single-handedly ruins what should have been one of the happiest days in Cheryl's life.

Malik finally gives up and drives away. Fresh sobbing comes from Cheryl as she watches him leave, knowing her future has just died an untimely death. Malik has the unpleasant task of explaining to his family and friends what has happened, and why the engagement party is not going to happen. Hours later, when she is sure that it was too late for the party to happen, Mama relinquishes her post at the door, throwing the keys on the floor and telling us to do whatever the hell we want to do. Quickly we grab the keys, open the door and fly out of the house, trying to understand what has happened. Curious neighbors stand around wondering what will happen next. Taking Nadine with her, Cheryl runs to Malik's home seeking what she hopes to be refuge from this craziness. From her upstairs bedroom window ,mother sees Cheryl going down the street. She runs down the stairs and out the door yelling her name. Cheryl turns around and Mama shouts. "I don't care where you go, but leave that child right here." Cheryl, at this point, wants nothing to do with her, much less leave her child who is already upset.

Turning on her heels, Cheryl continues walking away. Mother rushes up behind her and tries grabbing Nadine's hand, as she tries to pull her out of her mother's arms. Cheryl whirls around, holding her child closer to her chest. A fight begins between mother and daughter for Nadine, who is bawling at the top of her voice. Mama pulls at Nadine's flailing legs, and Cheryl hangs on to her for dear life. I run to my sister's aid. In the middle of the street, with all the neighbors looking on we wrestle with our mother to loosen her grip on Nadine. She holds on with the grip of a lioness, and Cheryl hugs her crying baby to her chest, crushing the very air out of her lungs. Everyone is screaming at the top of his voice, creating one of the most disgraceful scenes I have ever witnessed.

What a disgrace! I will never be able to hold up my head in the neighborhood again. A street fight with my mother. What has befallen this family?

I do not want to go back into the house; it no longer feels like home, more like a dungeon in which evil dwells. I take my children by their hands and we walk as far away as we can. My girls, between sobs, ask for Nadine. "She's with her mom." I tell them. "You'll see her later." As dusk turns to dark, I know I have to retrace my steps and take the children home. Walking back, I'm deep in thought. I know that my time in this place is over. I can no longer continue living with my children under these volatile and unstable circumstances. Mother has locked herself in her bedroom chanting and praying at the top of her voice, for the death and destructing of all of us. With tear-stained faces Cheryl returns, taking Nadine to bed with her.

At sunrise the following morning, Mama walks into the backyard pulls out her breasts and begins beating on them. She holds a lit match to the nipples; while imploring God to rid her of her afflictions. The situation is hopeless. Watching her, I come to the conclusion that it's too risky to leave the children with her during the days, so I decide to take time off from work to find a new place to live. There is no telling what a crazed mind will do next. That her reasoning makes sense to no one but herself is irrelevant.

Cheryl is miserable. No amount of support and compassion has been able to ebb the flow of tears. She has been humiliated by her mother in front of the person she loves, and now to make things worse, his family, after hearing what had happened to prevent the engagement, is adamant that Malik stop seeing her. They are furious about the wasted money, embarrassed about having to explain the situation to their family and friends, and have given Malik an ultimatum to stop seeing the daughter of a crazy woman or else. I am deeply embarrassed. I don't want to be in the house, and I am too ashamed to venture outside of it. The whispers of the neighbors can be heard when I walk down the streets. I hang my head low with shame. Like the trooper I have learned to become, I continue with my life, not knowing what will happen next.

The days drag on. Tempers flare easily, and the atmosphere is thick with impending doom. We know something else just as awful is going to happen, but have no idea of what, when, or on whom the hatchet will fall. If I could have been given one small peek into the future I would have been better prepared for the next tragedy.

Chapter Fourteen

HOMELESS

Still reeling from the events of the previous week, we speak in hushed voices about the total embarrassment which took place. We are still trying to comfort Cheryl, but to no avail. Malik has been forbidden by his family to see her, and she is devastated. The children have been traumatized. Nadine huddles close to her mother, afraid to leave her side.

Norris comes by and I jump into his car, begging him to drive away as fast as far away as possible from 26 Defoe Avenue. Even then, I am careful to avoid mentioning what transpired over the weekend, fearful that he will sever the relationship with the daughter of a crazed woman. If he makes that choice, no one will blame him. After all, why would anyone choose to associate themselves with the likes of me?

I begin asking co-workers if they know of an apartment for rent. My brother has settled into my former apartment and I don't think it's fair to disrupt his life asking him to give it back to me, besides, I want to get out of the neighborhood. This is no longer a place to be. My children need to be in a better environment away from the stigma of being related to Mrs. McLaren.

I don't have just any mother to contend with – I have a hateful, jealous, crazy person. I survived my childhood. Now I have to survive her into adulthood. To do so is easier than before; all I have to do is get out of her house

The tension in the household is tighter than a tight rope and the silence is deafening. Curiously, I wait to see if she will get dressed and go to church on Sabbath, pretending to be pious, good and holy. Sure enough, she does. Dressed in white to sing in the choir, she clamps her hat on her head, secures her Bible under her arms, picks up her purse, stuffs her feet into her white pumps, and without speaking a word to any of us, waltzes out the front door to church. If God was like man, he would smite her. But He doesn't, and I know that my freedom will last only for a few hours. She'll return soon.

I tell Norris not to pick me up over the weekend. I'm not in the mood to go drinking and dancing: I have a serious decision to make. In her absence, my sisters and I talk freely. Planning to find a house to rent, we will move into it sharing the expenses. Anton will remain at home. This sounds like a good idea. Tomorrow, we'll buy a newspaper and search the classifieds. With a plan in place, some of our gloom disappears and a pinpoint of light appears at the far end of a very long and dark tunnel.

After completing my chores on Sunday morning, I prepare to walk out to the corner shop to buy a newspaper. I hear voices in the living room and go to see who is here. It's Lester, our older brother. In her words, Mama tells him how we tried beating her out of the house the previous weekend. She turns everything around, making herself the victim of our terror. She tells her son that she had to grab a machete to protect herself from us because we wanted to capture her house so that we and our father could live in it after putting her out.

"That's not true," I interrupt. "We were trying to go to Cheryl's engagement party and she locked us all in, including Cheryl so that none of us could go. She kept threatening to kill anyone of us who came close enough to the door. Malik came to get Cheryl and she wouldn't let her go, she even threatened to kill him if he came through the gate. Now Malik has stopped talking to Cheryl because his family told him that if he continues seeing her, they'll have nothing to do with him."

"Mama came to me crying that she is fearful for her life and afraid to sleep at nights because you, Marcia, have threatened to kill her in her sleep. She asked me to come here today to remove all of you from her house so she can sleep at nights and be at peace."

"Lester, Mama is lying. She's the one who keeps telling us that she's going to pour hot oil in our ears while we're asleep. She's the one who went crazy last Saturday night, bringing down disgrace on the family when she ran down the street after Cheryl grabbing Nadine from her while screaming at the top of her lungs."

"I don't care what happened. The only thing I know is that Mama came to me crying that she is afraid to live in her own home with all of you here so I'm here to put you all out of her house."

"What do you mean you are here to put us out of the house? This is where we live. We have no place to go."

"That is going to be your problem. All of you need to leave now."

"Are you crazy? Leave to where?"

"All of you get out of here now. Mama wants all of you out and I'm here to help her do it. Get out of here. Get your junk and your pickneys and get out of here. This poor woman has worked all her life and now she can't sleep in peace in her own house. None of you is going to spend one more night in here."

"This is our father's house. Mama has never worked one day in her life outside of the house, our father has worked all of his life to buy and pay for this house. You can't throw us out. We have a right to be here if we want to be here. She has already thrown out Daddy. He was like a squatter in his own home. And now she wants to throw us out. And who are you? Where did you come from, ordering us out of here? You don't know anything about what happened. We did nothing to her. This is not fair."

"Marcia, I'm not here to argue with any of you. I'm just telling you that if you don't get out of here, I will personally throw each one of you out."

"You are going to have to throw me out then, because I am not leaving. This is my father's house."

Screaming at me to get out of his mother's house Lester moves towards me. Mother begins laughing, egging him on.

"Throw all of them out! Get them out of my house! I don't want them here. Let them go find their pa and live with him. I hate all of them; get them all out of my sight. See, I have help. You all thought you could beat me out of here, but who's laughing now. Ha ha! Get out of my house you bastards."

Lester moves through the house, grabbing our stuff and throwing them outside. Mother runs upstairs, empties our drawers and yanks our clothing from the closets, throwing armsfull of clothing outside. We're screaming, the children are crying, Mama is singing, and Lester is telling us to hurry up and get out.

Within one hour of Lester's arrival, all the earthly possessions of eight people are strewn all over the front yard and into the street. He and our mother push us out the door and through the gate into the street. Eight of us stand there with no idea what to do. Mother picks up the clothing that has fallen in the yard, throwing them at our feet, locking the gate with a padlock. She then goes back into the house, slamming and locking the door, laughing hysterically at the plight of her children.

Should I have fought back? Should I have hit my mother, pushing her out of the way? Maybe I should have grabbed my stuff from her or push her down the stairs? I can't fight Lester; he's much bigger and stronger than all of us put together. I didn't hit, push or curse my mother. Instead I tried defending myself to my brother, but he wouldn't listen to me and didn't believe me. Instead, he believed Mama's lies. Now I am standing on the street corner with three children to provide shelter and security for. What am I going to do? The neighbors are all out looking, talking and laughing at us. We ask each other the question on every mind: What are we going to do? There are no definite answers.

The five McLaren children have become homeless. We have no extended family. Mother has carefully disassociated us from all family members in another attempt to ensure secrecy. When I tried to make contact with one of her sisters who lives nearby, she tells me, "I want nothing to do with Vira's children. I have nothing against you guys, but if we build a relationship, your mother will find out and I do not want her in my life." I don't know where to find our father, and our only grandparent, the venerable Miss Ruby has no interest in us.

Years ago, Miss Ruby had showed up at the house in a state of anger. That was the first and only time I met my grandmother. An argument ensued between her and Mama, and much to my surprise, this petite woman of advanced years jumped up on a chair, and swiftly and resolutely slapped the face of her 50+-year-old daughter in the presence of her husband and children. The sound of the contact with flesh echoed through the room, followed by her warning.

"Gal, who do you think you are talking to? Do you think you are too old for me to whip your ass? Don't let me have to return here to fix your business. You can be as old as a horse, but until the day you die, you will always be a child to me."

This was the first time in my life that I witnessed my mother being humiliated. With mouth wide open, I stared at the scene between mother and daughter as it unfolded before my eyes. I made no comment, just watched in awe.

What are we going to do? There is no one to call, no place to go. The children are crying. We are all crying. The neighbors are sympathetic, but no one dares to offer help. Mama will probably burn to the ground the home of anyone who takes in or offers assistance to even the smallest child.

Chapter Fifteen

FINDING REFUGE

What a calamity. Woefully, we survey our belongings, and the enormity of the crisis which has befallen us becomes clear. We have to find shelter, the children have to be cared for, and night is quickly approaching. We begin tossing ideas around to each other. Who can we call, where can we go? Located at the end of the block is a pay phone. We search through our purses for address books and phone numbers of people whom we may be able to spend a few days with until we sort ourselves out.

Leaving everything where it lays on the street, the band of eight walks to the pay phone. Bridget calls a friend who shows up shortly afterwards to get her. Janice walks a few blocks to friends in the neighborhood asking for their assistance. They agreed to let her stay with them and show up with bags helping to pack her belonging into them. Cheryl, swallowing her pride, walks to Malik's parent's home. She tells them what has happened to us and asked for accommodations. They grudgingly tell her they could let her sleep on the couch, but her child was not welcome, they had no room for a child and neither were they prepared to have a small child crying in their home. I tell her to go ahead and I'll take care of Nadine.

Anton has no one to call, no place to go. Much to my chagrin, I have no choice but to call my godfather. I tell him what has happened and ask if I could stay there with the three children. He struggles with the decision, but eventually agrees, telling me that the living arrangement cannot last long. I promise to get out as soon as possible. He tells me to take a taxi and come up. I take Anton along with me.

Before separating, we kiss one another, holding on long and hard, not wanting to sever our bond. Our lives are teetering on the brink of disaster. We have no idea what is going to happen to any of us. On this fateful Sunday evening in 1981, my family is irrevocably broken apart. We struggle to let go of one another. When we can, we go our separate ways, crying our hearts out for our uncertain future, for our separation, and for our shattered lives. We become separated from one another's presence, but never from our hearts.

That Sunday afternoon was the last day that I lived in that house. It was the last morning I woke up in that house, the last day I put a glass of water to my lips in that house. I will never tread the stairs leading to the bedrooms again. The place, which had housed me for 14 years, becomes a forbidden dungeon in the space of one hour. Never again will I sit down to a meal at the dining table. Before driving away for the last time, I decided that I will never return to this place. I purpose in my heart that day that I will never speak to her again. Mother has gotten her wish and succeeded in getting us out of her house. Now I will leave her to enjoy her own misery.

The taxi stops at the gate. I get out, opening the gate so the driver could drive up to the back door. With a strained smile, Uncle Nowington greets us, Anton is helping me unload the taxi. My godfather asks if the cab will be taking my brother back down the hill. I lie, telling him yes, he had only accompanied me to help with the children. I'll have to devise a plan to keep him here. Living in his home is just as bad as where we came from. But we have no choice. The children have been settled down and I sit down to talk with him. He wants to know what happened at home to cause the breakdown, I try reliving the episode, but it's too fresh and way too painful to relive. I gloss over the details.

Tentatively, I ask if Anton could also be allowed to spend the night. Uncle Nowington refuses to harbor another stray. My brain shifts into gear. If Anton leaves, he has no place to go and there is no way I'm going to allow my young brother to wander the streets. Its getting dark, I know he expects Anton to leave. I excuse myself to go get him to say his goodbyes. Very quietly, I give him instructions,

"Come and say goodbye to Uncle Nowington, walk down the driveway, go out the gate and pretend to lock it behind you. Walk around the other side of the house, re-entering from the unlocked back door. If the dogs start barking, just slip into the chauffeur's room, wait there until I come to get you."

For weeks he lives like a fugitive hiding, from the authorities, sleeping in the gardener's or maid's quarters. We pass food to him through the iron gate, or if it's safe, he eats his meals at the kitchen table. The helpers have been entrusted to keep our secret. He is miserable, but at least there is a roof over his head and food in his stomach.

It's difficult getting the girls to settle down in their new surroundings. It's hard keeping them quiet, trying not to upset the peace and tranquility of the household. I am frazzled, my patience is wearing thin, but I take deep breaths, brush away the tears from my eyes and keep going. Monday morning the chauffeur is given a new job, that of transporting the children to and from school. I do as much for them as possible, not wanting to impose upon the time of the help to care for the girls. For the most part they are happy. They learn to play quietly, especially when Uncle Nowington or guests are in the home. I watch over them like a hawk, making it my mission to be present at all times when he talks with them. They are never left home alone in his care and Jessica, who is seven, is instructed to tell me if he ever touches her anywhere except on her hands. They are told never to sit on his lap and never ever to enter his bedroom.

Maybe I'm paranoid, but I don't care. I know first-hand what he is capable of. I promise myself to use one of his own guns (which he has taught me to fire) to kill him if he ever touches any of these innocent girls. He keeps his filthy hands off them, and we make the most of the situation, being grateful for a place to lay our heads at night. After a while, Anton begins staying with friends from church and stops coming by daily. I miss him terribly. He is my only link with my family. But I'm happy that he has found a place to call home, even for a short time.

I communicate with my sisters as often as possible. No one is sleeping on the streets, and although no situation is ideal, we are all working with what is available. Cheryl misses her daughter and visits on most weekends, always with Nadine screaming for her mother, becoming hysterical when she leaves. Malik did not abandon Cheryl after all. About six months later, against the wishes of his parents, they rent an apartment and begin living together, and Nadine goes to live with them.

Anton visits Daddy at his place of employment, telling him what has happened. Daddy sends word to us that he is well. He has been staying with old friends, and he misses us terribly, but is trying to endure the hardships. A few months later he sends news that his eyes are bothering him, his blood pressure has escalated, and he has been diagnosed with diabetes. My father is ill, and I don't even know where he lives. The very thought of him suffering or being in need, with none of his children around to even hand him a glass of water has me crying on my pillow at nights, and with every thought of the safety and living conditions of my sisters and brother, resentment rises up in me. With every memory of how she has torn our lives apart, I hate Mama more. I hate the memory of her; I hate the fact that she has given birth to me. I hate what she has done to me throughout my life; I hate what she has allowed to be done to me. My hate grows so strong that if I hear that she died, I'll probably not attend her funeral. I never want to see her again.

She has finally gotten her desire: she managed to chase all of us out of the house. Now she's living large, doing as she pleases, enjoying the comforts of her paradise by herself. No one speaks to her. Daddy and his five children are out of the house, which he had worked hard to purchase and pay for. How unfair can life be?

Loathing is a mild description of what I feel for her. The mention of her name causes revulsion to rise up in my stomach. I promise myself never to have anything to do with her ever again. If she needed help and depended upon me to provide it, she would die before I would stretch my hands out to her. If she depended on me to make it possible for her to see my children again she would go to her grave without them passing before her eyes. I resolve in my heart that the remainder of my days will be spent without her. As far as I'm concerned, she is already dead. I'm motherless.

Three months later, Norris, who visits often, tells me that he has decided to permanently migrate to the United States. He has already made arrangements for the sale of his businesses, and land he owns in St. Catherine. His eldest son will occupy his home. He promises that his leaving will not be the end of our relationship; he was only going ahead to make plans for us to join him soon in America.

The night prior to his departure he visits to say goodbye. I will miss him. Since taking up residence on the hill we, had not been able to spend any time together. I had no baby sitters and would never consider leaving my children in the care of my godfather for even one minute, therefore all social activities had been curtailed. He promises that his migration to the USA is the first step in getting us out of Jamaica. He promises to get an apartment, find employment and make preparation for us to become a family. He tells me to get the children's passports, so we will be ready to join him there. He also promised to call with a telephone number so we can keep in touch. I believe him, placing all my trust in him to help us out of our predicament.

He keeps his word, calling me the following day to give me his telephone number. We talk frequently, making plans to be reunited. He tells me he has rented a room in the home of a woman named Bessie. He says he had told her about me, even asked her to take messages from me if I called when he was absent. She has promised to do so.

This arrangement is working fine, until about four months later. His calls are coming more infrequently, and the conversation is strained, often ending within a few minutes.

Wondering why no calls had come from him for an entire week, I decide to place a call to him on the weekend. Sunday afternoon, I dial the number and Bessie answers the telephone. When I identified myself, her friendly tone changed to one of cold controlled fury.

"Hello Bessie. How are you?"

"I am fine. What do you want?"

"May I speak to Norris?"

"Norris is not home."

"Can you tell him I called, and ask him to give me a call back."

"I will tell him no such thing and I do not want you calling my home anymore."

I'm not sure of what I heard.

"Excuse me, what did you say?" Loudly she repeats her statement.

"Norris is not home and I do not want you calling my house anymore, your calls are no longer welcome."

"Woman, do you know who I am?"

"I know who you used to be. You have been replaced, he is no longer interested in you, and his interest has shifted to me, so stop calling my house."

"Go to hell, you bitch."

"No sweetheart, you go to hell. Norris is now mine so stop calling him."

I slam the telephone down, and that was the last time my fingers dialed that number. I wait by the phone for him to call and apologise for what she had said – even if it's a lie. I need him to tell me something, but no calls come. I guess she had been right after all. I have become a used-to-be.

I throw myself into caring for my little girls to fill the void left by Norris. My mind constantly swirls around him and the lost relationship. He was my only hope, my lifeline, and my ticket to freedom. "What's a girl to do?" The man has made his choice. Within a few months, our lives become bearable to a point. We continue living with my godfather but I'm desperately trying to get out of his house. He no longer bothers me at nights – he has a live-in lover and many other women and young girls satisfying his sexual appetite. But I need to establish my own household with the girls. They need stability, and I need peace of mind.

There is no one in Jamaica for me to turn to. I have four older sisters living in Canada. Can they help me? I have not communicated with them since they visited when I was pregnant with Jessica, six years ago. I rummage through my old purses, looking for a telephone number. Thank you, Lord, here is the number, now please let it still be her number. I ask for and receive permission to place a call to Canada, the answering machine comes on and I leave a message for my sister.

One day, about one week later, I'm called to the telephone. It's one of my sisters from Canada on the line. She asks what's been going on with the family. I tell her what has happened. Of course, Mama had given her an entirely different version of the entire incident telling that I had attacked her with a knife, trying to beat her out of her house so I could capture it and live there with my man and children. She knows mother's tendencies to lie and distort the truth, so thankfully she believes me that I had no such intentions, and that is not what happened. Before the call ends my sister asks the most important question I have ever been asked in my entire life.

"Would you like to come to Canada?"

Would I like to go to Canada? "Yes, yes, I want to come to Canada. Will you please, please help me? I must get out of here, I must save my children, I will be eternally grateful to you if you will help me, please!" She promises to talk to the others and get back to me soon.

"O God please let them decide to help me, I must get out of here, please God, please let them help me."

Soon cannot come fast enough. Every time the telephone rings I jump to it. Is this the call? I'm walking on clouds, just the thought of getting away. Plans form in mind of how it's going to be for the girls and myself. I'm building castles in the air, anything, anywhere, anyplace, will be better than where we are now. I keep praying for help to save my children.

Two weeks later, the long-awaited call comes. My heart skips a beat as I listen to the plans which have been made for me to get to Canada. An invitation letter will be sent to me, and immigration regulations are explained. I am ready to do whatever is necessary. Then the bad news comes. My children will have to be left behind; it's impossible for me to take them with me. Canadian residence has to be established first. I remember when Lynette left, leaving her three children behind, now they have been happily reunited. Can I leave my children behind? With whom will I leave them?

If my children have to be left with my mother, my feet will never leave the shores of Jamaica. We will all remain right here together and continue suffering. They are never going to be placed in her care, not over my dead body. But who am I going to leave them with? The process begins, in a couple weeks the promised documents arrive. I have to make adequate plans for my children. I tell my godfather about my sister's invitation and that I have accepted the proposal. He thinks it's a good decision and gives me his blessings. Tearfully I sit my two daughters down to tell them what was going on. The thought of leaving them is so overwhelming that I almost abandon the idea. But it's the only way out. We have to sacrifice something to achieve what I've been hoping for. A better life for us.

My very being is torn apart as I struggle to make plans to leave my children behind. They cry constantly, afraid of what they know is coming. I talk with them often about the trip, it's heart-wrenching. If I could leave them with my sisters, the departure will be easier on all of us, but thanks to a crazy woman, no one is in a position to keep the girls for me. My sisters and I meet in the mall to discuss the problem. I desperately want to go, but what will become of my children? We put our heads together mapping out a workable plan. One of the suggestion is that I approach Jessica's father and his wife, asking them to care for her. She had spent weekends with them, and likes his new wife who has no children of her own and treats her like her own daughter. I decide to ask Chad's mother to care for Nia.

Both families are presented with my situation and I ask for help with the children until I'm able to get them to Canada. Jessica's father and wife readily agree to care for her. They will love to have her join their family. Jessica is willing to live with them until Mommy comes back for her. Nia's fate proves to be a little more daunting, her grandmother works full time. Chad still lives at home, but doesn't want to commit to taking responsibility for her. She is four years old, and needs a mother's care. My heart is breaking, but I've fixed my eyes on the end result. Getting us out of the country. This is terrible; I realize that it's only going to get harder before it gets better. I keep pressing on; I must find someone safe with whom to leave Nia.

A friendship had formed between Miss Baker, Nia's school's principal and myself. One morning during a conversation, I mention my opportunity and desire to leave Jamaica for Canada, telling her about the dilemma of having no one with whom to leave Nia. She offers to care for my baby for me. I'm surprised at her response, questioning the reason behind her offer. She explains that she now has two children in her care whose mothers have migrated to America. She assures me that she has the space and will be more than willing to care for Nia, whom she loves.

This ray of hope is discussed at length with my sisters and with Nia. Although she is only four years old, we give her a voice in where and with whom she will live. Naturally, she prefers to be with her mom, but she is able to grasp the meaning of what we have been explaining to her. A week later, my girls and I make a trip to visit and explore the home in which Nia may be placed. Everything seems okay. She'll share a room with a five-year-old girl whose mother is in the United States. There will be no problems getting her to school; this is the principal's home.

This is far from an ideal situation. My sisters and I continue talking, contemplating our options. Regardless of how nice this woman appears to be, she is still a stranger. Can I trust her with the life of my precious little girl? My sisters and I make three more trips to Miss Baker, taking the girls with us, trying to make certain that Nia will be all right there. Finally after extensive talking, asking questions, surveying the visitors to the home, watching the interaction between Nia, and the other children, we make the decision. Nia will be left in the care of Miss Baker.

My airline ticket arrives in the mail. My departure is two weeks away. My stomach falls to my feet. While I want to go, reality is staring me in the face and I have to step up to the plate. I think of abandoning the entire idea telling my children and sisters that I have chosen to remain with my children. But remaining in Jamaica will only mean having more children for another loser, getting into relationships for the wrong reasons, wasting my life away. No, as hard as this is going to be, I have to go through with the plans in place, for my children's sake. I brought them into the world and I'll do anything to provide for them. We're all going to suffer, but leaving Jamaica is the first step in the long journey to provide a better life for them. I will go through with it.

Anton and I take my girls to visit Daddy and tell him of my plans. It breaks my heart to see him in a state I have never seen him in before. His sight has deteriorated quite rapidly, to the point where he needs assistance moving around the house. He recognizes us, but says we appear as blurs in his vision. He is overwhelmed with joy to have his grandchildren around him. We talk about our lives, without mother and all the hardships we have endured. Before leaving his side I promise to bring him off the island, if not permanently then for a vacation, somewhere in the future. Hours later, we say goodbye, crying on each other's shoulders. Before leaving, I tell my Daddy how much I love him, assuring him that I will never forget him. I cry all the way home, aching for my Daddy's situation and hating mother for putting him in it.

Little did I know that was the last time I would lay eyes on my beloved father alive or dead. I have never seen my dad again. The hole in my heart is so deep that nothing have or will ever be able to fill it up, that special place reserved for him can never be filled with all the love in the world. I still miss him and will never forget the only person who has ever unconditionally, unreservedly loved me.

Chapter Sixteen

DAWNING OF A NEW DAY

ecember 2, 1982. Christmas season is approaching. The attitudes of many change from sour to cheerful, the stores are decorated with Christmas trappings, and the entire atmosphere is charged with expectancy and good cheer. But there are no festive feelings in the hearts of my children, my sisters nor myself. Today is my departure day. I have lived through many difficult days in my 25 years, but today is the worst one I will have to endure. My girls are glued to my side, refusing to be separated from me. My sisters will take them to their respective places from the airport. They had gathered by our sides to help us deal with the changes. The girls' bags have been packed and are loaded into the trunk of a friend's car, my bags are in the trunk of another friend's car. We hug and say our last goodbyes to Uncle Nowington. The gravel crunches beneath the wheels of the cars, as they slowly roll down the driveway onto the street for the sad trip to the airport.

My children ride with me, crying during the entire trip. They know that this ride will end in separation. They cling to each other, knowing that in a couple hours, not only are they going to lose their mother, they are also going to be losing each other. How their young hearts must ache. Their lives have been shattered to pieces – they will no longer have each other to talk or play with, and worst of all, no mommy to love and care for them. To make matters worse, I have no idea when we will be reunited. My poor children: how are they going to endure their losses? Everyone dear to them has disappeared from their lives.

At the airport, they become inconsolable almost to the point of hysteria. My only choices are to get on the plane, or turn around and return from whence we came. Somehow I have a feeling that we will not be welcomed back in Uncle Nowington's home. He had grown tired of us. With super-human strength, we manage to dry our eyes, remove the bags from the trunk of the car, and follow the signs leading to Air Canada. My family enters the airport, venturing as far as security allows. We spend more tearful minutes in long hugs and wet kisses. With no more time to spare, I say a final goodbye, turn and walk away from my children.

With red swollen eyes, and a heart about to burst, I turn to give a final wave, blowing kisses and mouthing I love you. Drying the tears from my eyes I head for the terminal. The passengers are being boarded so there is no more time to procrastinate. The die has been cast.

At that time, boarding an airplane in Jamaica requires the passengers to exit the building, walk onto the tarmac, then climb a stairway to board the plane. The good thing about this is that loved ones have a final opportunity to watch you board the plane from the waving gallery. You can take an additional minute to turn around for one last wave before you are swallowed up by the confines of the plane. As I approach the door of the plane, my family shouts my name. I turn around and stand there waving and throwing kisses to my children and sisters for a minute, while others push past me.

I find my seat. Thank God, I have the window. Gazing out the window, locating and watching my children requires all my effort to keep from screaming. I know that they are crying, I can almost hear them screaming for mommy. Panic rises up in my throat.

What have I done? This was a bad decision. Who is going to care for my children? No one can love them as dearly as I do. Who is going to tuck them in at nights, comb their hair, and make their favorite meals? When am I going to see my children again?

"O my God, help me. I have abandoned my children. I can't do this; I have to go to them. I know they're crying. I can see my sisters with their arms around them comforting them, I can hear them calling my name, they are wondering why have I abandoned them, but I have to go."

I have to get off the plane; I can't go through with this. Nausea rises up in the back of my throat threatening to spill out onto the person sitting next to me. Swallowing heavily I turn to the woman in the next seat.

"Excuse me I need to get off the plane. My children need me."

I gather my purse and hand luggage together while attempting to unbuckle the seat belt. With a look of pure pity, my seating companion says to me, "Is this your first time leaving the Island?'

"No but this time is different," I stammer

"Are you leaving family behind?"

"My two daughters, sisters and brothers."

"How long will you be gone?"

"I don't know. I miss them so much I want to go back, but there is nothing to go back to. This is an opportunity to help them, but I don't want to leave them."

"Don't worry, they'll be fine. Many of us have had to leave our children behind at first, but it will all work out in the end, you'll see. Just relax and enjoy the trip," she advises. "You are going to provide a better life for them. They'll appreciate this later, and you'll be glad you were strong enough to do what is best for them now."

Enjoy the trip? Is she crazy? My only enjoyments are my children in my arms, and now they were standing on a waving gallery weeping for me. They are my entire life. What am I going to do without them? What are they going to do without me?

Waves of emotion wash over me. I want to scream my head off, but the situation allows no such display. In an attempt to control myself, I press my face into the window trying to catch one last glimpse of my family while hiding my tears from my seating companion and the eyes of the other passengers.

As the door of the plane closes and the wheels begin moving, I strain my neck to watch in desperation as my children and family wave the plane out of sight. I know they are hurting. I know that my children are crying their hearts out. I know they want their mummy back. I feel like a traitor, as if I had betrayed them. Silently, I beg God to take care of them. This has to be done. I have to provide a better life for them. I'll get a job, send money back to care for them and as soon as possible bring them to Canada to join me. My other sisters have done it, now it's my turn to do it for my children. These thoughts help me to retain my sanity. This is for my children; I will do anything for them. This separation will not be for long. By the grace of God, we'll be back together soon. This is for my children.

My mother has not been told about my departure from Jamaica and that's the way I want it to be. I have not spoken to her since that fateful day and have no intentions of doing so.

New hatred rises up in me for her. It's her fault that I am in this situation. She is responsible for displacing us to the point of dissolution. I don't want to leave my children; they need me to protect them from the likes of Uncle Nowington and their grandmother. Fresh tears course down my cheeks. A sob escapes my lips and my hand covers my mouth. Unable to conceal it my inner agony turns into soul racking sobs. A piece of tissue is handed to me, but it's not enough to stem the torrent of tears. My heart has been broken into a million pieces and scattered over the Caribbean Sea, as the nose of the airplane lifts into the sky, taking me thousands of miles from my two precious little daughters.

When will I see my children again? Frantically I begin praying, "Oh Dear God, I love my children more than life itself. Please watch over them and keep them safe. They are very precious to me and they are all I have. You gave them to me for a reason, and I have to provide for them. So far I have done a lousy job. Now they have been left behind in the hands of strangers. I miss them. They are going to suffer and cry for me, but I must do this so I can provide for them. Please allow them to be properly cared for and keep them from harm and danger. Open a way for me in Canada, and make it possible for us to be reunited in the very near future. Amen."

I feel the hand of my seating companion on my arm as she offers me another tissue, trying to reassure me that it is going to be alright. I take the tissue, but don't bother to dry my tears, this is too much. I don't care who knows that I am crying. I lean my head back on the head rest, trying to feel the presence of my children with me, I wrap my arms around my body, holding my girls close to me in my mind.

With a sigh of helplessness, I exhale, closing my eyes, rolling my head from side to side, openly crying.

The plane is in the air, on its way to Toronto, Canada. In four hours, I will land in a foreign country. What am I going to find there? How am I going to deal with the snow, which I have never seen? O my God, what will I do if there is no one at the airport to pick me up?

With these and many other questions on my mind, I am lulled into a fitful sleep, praying and dreaming of my girls. I am jarred awake as the plane goes through a bumpy patch. I rub the tears from my eyes as they escape and roll down my cheeks. My heart that had been torn into a million pieces finds a thread of hope. While praying, a sense of peace fills my heart, as the words of comfort from the scriptures, which I had learned many years ago fill my mind. Repeating them to myself I feel comforted. Even in my despair, I have been given a thread of hope on which to hang on to.

This is what will keep me going until I am reunited with my children. I have entrusted them into the hands of God, and He has filled my heart with hope and peace. As the plane soars towards its destination, I keep my heart lifted up to God. The tears keep coming, as I am still worried about my precious daughters. My favorite Bible verse keeps playing in my head. I know that God is with me and He will take care of my girls. When I am afraid, I will hold these words of promise close to my heart, until I hold my children in my arms again:

"Fear not for I am with you; be not dismayed; for I am
your God. I will strengthen you, yes, I will help you, yes,
I will uphold you with the right hand of my righteousness."
Isaiah 41:10 (KJV)

* * *

Have faith in God, because He loves and cares for you.
Have faith in God.
He will help, strengthen, provide and keep you.
Have faith in God. There is nothing He cannot do
Have faith in God. He will see you through
Have faith, dear friends, in GOD.